ANF-
HIST

Evacuees

This book is dedicated to
all who have suffered as a result of war

Evacuees

Children's Lives on the WW2 Home Front

Gillian Mawson

PEN & SWORD
HISTORY

First published in Great Britain in 2014 by
Pen & Sword History
an imprint of
Pen & Sword Books Ltd
47 Church Street
Barnsley
South Yorkshire
S70 2AS

Copyright © Gillian Mawson 2014

ISBN 978 1 78383 153 1

Typeset in Ehrhardt by
Mac Style Ltd, Bridlington, East Yorkshire
Printed and bound in the UK by CPI Group (UK) Ltd, Croydon,
CRO 4YY

Pen & Sword Books Ltd incorporates the imprints of Pen & Sword
Archaeology, Atlas, Aviation, Battleground, Discovery, Family
History, History, Maritime, Military, Naval, Politics, Railways, Select,
Transport, True Crime, and Fiction, Frontline Books, Leo Cooper,
Praetorian Press, Seaforth Publishing and Wharncliffe.

For a complete list of Pen & Sword titles please contact
PEN & SWORD BOOKS LIMITED
47 Church Street, Barnsley, South Yorkshire, S70 2AS, England
E-mail: enquiries@pen-and-sword.co.uk
Website: www.pen-and-sword.co.uk

Contents

Introduction

I have always had a passionate interest in social history and during 2013 I started to collect stories of evacuation from those who spent the war years away from home as evacuees in England, Northern Ireland, Scotland and Wales. Within this book, 100 of these moving stories are accompanied by photographs, many of which have been rescued from old suitcases and attics.

Prior to commencing work on Evacuees, I spent four years interviewing hundreds of evacuees from Guernsey for my first book, *Guernsey Evacuees: The Forgotten Evacuees of the Second World War*. Over 17,000 evacuees fled from Guernsey to England in June 1940, just weeks before the five-year occupation of their island by German forces began. Sadly, many of those I interviewed have since died and, in common with the aims of the Evacuees Reunion Association, I feel that it is vital that the memories of Second World War evacuees are recorded now, before they are lost for ever.

During the past year, I have interviewed people who were evacuated within Britain as part of Operation Pied Piper and discovered the stories of others who sought sanctuary in Britain from war-torn Europe. I also came across the memories of those who, in 1940, found refuge in England from British territories, like Guernsey, Jersey, Alderney and Gibraltar the majority were not sent to the safety of the countryside.

The aim of this book is to provide a particularly memorable incident or story from each evacuee's reminiscences, encapsulating their personal experience of evacuation. These are presented together with a wartime family photograph, allowing an intimate glimpse into 100 lives affected by war. Several of the evacuees did not have the luxury of a camera during the war, but local history societies, newspapers and members of the public have kindly allowed me to use relevant photographs to illustrate their stories.

It was difficult to choose just one extract from each of these stories, as all represent a compelling and important part of British wartime history. Whilst preparing the stories for publication, however, it seemed natural to split them into five themes: 'Arrival and Departure' depicts the initial upheaval of evacuation; 'A Different World' reveals the culture shock for evacuees of finding themselves in a new environment, often completely dissimilar to their family home; in 'The Kindness of Strangers' stories focus on the bonds forged between evacuees and their foster parents; 'Suffer the Little Children' demonstrates that not all evacuees had positive wartime experiences; and 'We Were with the Children' tells the foster parents and care-givers' side of the story.

I have included stories from mothers and teachers who travelled with the schoolchildren and took on a huge responsibility. We tend to hear their stories far less often than those of child evacuees, yet they played a highly significant part in evacuation and it seems important to recognise this. In some cases schools were kept together as a unit and so the teachers became their pupils' guardians for five years, in a move unprecedented in educational history.

Another theme running through many stories shatters the myth that most evacuees were deprived city children who left the slums for pristine homes in the countryside. Many of the former evacuees I spoke to recall being shocked when they were placed in country cottages with no running water, gas or electricity. Others discovered that their foster families were less than enthusiastic about their presence and endured severe homesickness.

However different, all of the stories in this book underline one thing: that there is so much more to the history of evacuation during World War Two than the images of children arriving at railway stations, clutching gas masks and with labels tied to their coats, which have entered the popular imagination. Hopefully, this book, with its combination of stories and family photographs, will paint an intimate picture of the different ways in which the British people opened up their homes to evacuated children and adults during the dark days of the Second World War.

Gillian Mawson, 2014

Notice to Parents of Children Registered for Evacuation

READ THIS CAREFULLY — IT IS IMPORTANT.

1. The children will be taken to areas which the Government believe to be safer than the evacuating areas. Whilst no part of the country can be said to be absolutely safe, the children will have a better chance outside the towns. It is not possible to move all the children to places where they are unlikely to see anything of the war. The numbers to be moved are far too large for this, but the Government think that all the places to which children will be sent will be safer than the towns from which they will come.

2. The children will be accompanied by teachers. When they have been billeted, children will send to their parents the stamped postcard which they should take with them, giving their exact address.

3. HEALTH AND CLEANLINESS. First impressions are important, and it is essential that the people with whom our children are to be billeted should be impressed by their cleanliness. You should therefore do everything possible to ensure that your child goes away with clean clothes, clean hair and a clean body. Every Mother will wish her child to arrive at his new home in a state in which he will be welcomed.

All children will be carefully examined by the School Nurses and any instructions which are given regarding the children should be carefully carried out. If your child has sores of any kind or there is anything in connection with your child's health which you think she ought to know, don't hesitate to tell the Nurse. She is only too anxious to help you.

4. CLOTHING. The Heads of the Schools will have given you a list of clothing which it is desirable that your child should take. The following are the principal items which are given for your guidance :—

Gas Mask	Spare stockings or socks.
Identity Card.	House shoes or plimsolls.
Ration Book.	Warm coat or mackintosh.
Food for the day.	Toothbrush.
Change of underclothing.	Comb.
Night clothes.	Towel.
Handkerchiefs.	

The child should wear the overcoat or mackintosh and his thickest boots or shoes, and should be warmly clothed.

The luggage must not be more than the child can carry. Other clothes needed can be sent on later.

You will be responsible for renewing the child's clothing whilst away.

Gas masks should be slung over the shoulder and not carried in the luggage.

5. FOOD. As it may take some hours to reach the destination, every child must be given sufficient food for the day. The following items would make a good meal :—

Sandwiches (egg or cheese).	Barley sugar (rather than chocolate).
Packets of nuts or seedless raisins.	Apple; orange.
Dry biscuits (with little packets of cheese).	Liquids should not be carried by children.

6. LUGGAGE. The most suitable luggage carrier both for the journey and for use away is the rucksack. This is strapped on the back and leaves the arms free. If a rucksack is too expensive a haversack would be cheaper and is a good substitute.

All property belonging to a child should be marked with the child's name.

If you have not a haversack or small suitcase for your child, a pillow case makes a better carrier than a parcel. *Do not load up your child with parcels.*

7. LABELS. Two labels will be supplied by the school for your child. One should be affixed to his luggage, and the other, in the case of a girl, tied round her neck; and for a boy, fixed to the lapel of his jacket.

8. RATION BOOKS. Be sure that your child has his ration book with him. If pages of coupons out of his book have been deposited with retailers, ask for their return and pin the pages in the ration book.

Both the ration book and the identity card should be securely packed in the child's luggage and not given him to hold.

9. MEDICAL AND DENTAL TREATMENT. Unless I hear from you to the contrary it will be assumed that you give your consent to a doctor's or dentist's advice being carried out when your child is away from home.

10. It is realised that you will be anxious about your child, but I can assure you that as far as it is in the power of the Teachers, every care will be taken to look after him or her.

H. BOYES WATSON.
Chief Education Officer.

Official letter sent to parents notifying them of the arrangements for their child's evacuation. (*Courtesy of Dorothy Walsh née Reynolds*)

Chapter One

Arrivals and Departures:
Embarking on Evacuation

Guernsey evacuees John Helyer, Hazel Hall and June le Page leaving Bury, Lancashire in 1945. (*Courtesy of John Helyer*)

T hese stories focus on evacuees' poignant accounts of leaving their homes and arriving in evacuation reception areas. Some of the evacuees I interviewed still possess the evacuation instructions that they were given by their teachers. On the outbreak of war, parents were told to refer to the evacuation instructions and prepare a bag or rucksack containing the listed items that their child would need, should the call for evacuation arise.

Every day children would set off for school with their rucksack and a sandwich, in readiness for evacuation. Many children did not know if they would return home that day, whilst others had no real understanding of what evacuation actually meant. As they waved goodbye to their children each morning, parents had no idea whether they would return home from school that afternoon.

Schools held regular evacuation drills and children would spend hours, standing in lines in the playground, being counted, having their identity labels checked, and the contents of their bags examined. Some even practised the walk to their nearest railway station. Children were also told to bring a stamped postcard with their home address clearly written on it, so that they could send their new address to their parents once they reached their

TAKE THEM BACK!
TAKE THEM BACK!.
TAKE THEM BACK!..

DON'T do it, Mother —

LEAVE YOUR CHILDREN IN THE SAFER AREAS

ISSUED BY THE MINISTRY OF HEALTH

Government propaganda poster, urging mothers to have their children evacuated. (*Author's collection*)

new billet. They were instructed to write only cheerful messages that would not upset their parents, such as 'Dear Mum and Dad, I am in a good home here, and happy'.

According to James Roffey in *Send them to Safety*, this had tragic consequences for one little boy. The young evacuee posted a card home from his new billet, then went for a walk, but in the unfamiliar surroundings, he somehow fell into the canal, where he drowned. His family were advised of his death that evening, but the next morning his postcard arrived with its cheerful inscription, 'Dear Mum & Dad, I am very happy here, don't worry about me.'

In the early hours of 1 September 1939 the government's carefully devised plans for evacuation were put into operation, and the majority of the schools, teachers and escorts were moved before war was declared on 3 September 1939. As each school was evacuated, some parents found out at the very last moment, and ran to the railway station in order to say goodbye to their children. In some areas, such as Dagenham, long lines of children snaked through the streets, heading towards the ports where paddle steamers ships would transport them to safer areas.

As each school departed, a notice was hung upon its gates, announcing the destination to which the schoolchildren had been evacuated. When their children did not return home at the usual time, mothers gathered at the school gates to read these short, stark notices.

Meanwhile, when the evacuees arrived at the designated reception areas they were taken to public buildings, such as church halls and schools, where

A young evacuee finds comfort with her teddy bear beside a suitcase. (*Courtesy of the Kent Messenger Group*)

they were registered and given something to eat. Some received a carrier bag containing food items intended for their new foster parents. However, not all of the children understood this and many immediately began to consume the contents.

Finally, the evacuees were allocated to local families, usually in small groups or ones and twos. Siblings and, in some cases, mothers and their children, were often separated, and many must have spent that first night in a new place suffering badly from homesickness.

Saying Goodbye

Jean Noble, then aged seven, and her brother Bern, aged ten, were evacuated from Stoke Newington, London, to Reading in 1939.

'I arrived home one day from school and found we had a visitor, my grandmother's brother Frank, who lived with his daughter and her husband in Reading. To prevent us being billeted with strangers, they were offering to take us in. A few days later, we set off for Waterloo Railway Station with Mum.

'The noise in the concourse was tremendous, with hundreds of bewildered children, panicking parents and agitated teachers. The crush was frightening, with children trying to keep connected to their own little group while being pushed and jostled towards various railway platforms. I held tightly on to Mum's coat as she juggled with two suitcases and two children. Because we were not leaving with a school she was allowed to come onto the platform, where she reminded me

Jean Noble (left) and her brother Bern (right), were lucky enough to be evacuated to family members, rather than strangers. (*Courtesy of Jean Noble*)

that my brother was in charge. On reflection, for a ten-year-old he took his responsibility seriously and was stoical, not showing any sign of distress.

'Mum found us a carriage with seats by the window and waited on the platform, calling out last minute instructions to behave ourselves. Then, as the train started to pull away, I saw my mother's face crumple in abject misery and her floodgate of tears opened, which set me off and I grizzled for the rest of the journey. I realise now that we were lucky, because most of the other children on the train were travelling to some unknown destination in the West Country, and would be boarded with complete strangers.'

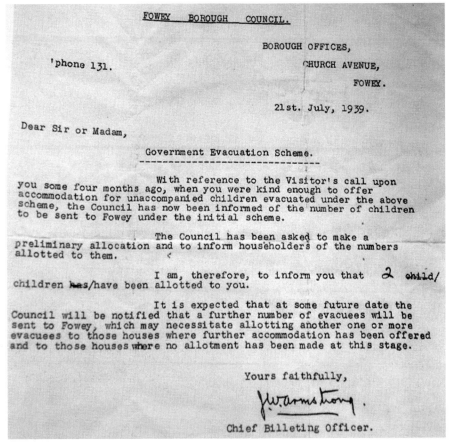

FOWEY   BOROUGH   COUNCIL.

BOROUGH OFFICES,
'phone 131.   CHURCH AVENUE,
FOWEY.

21st. July, 1939.

Dear Sir or Madam,

Government Evacuation Scheme.

With reference to the Visitor's call upon you some four months ago, when you were kind enough to offer accommodation for unaccompanied children evacuated under the above scheme, the Council has now been informed of the number of children to be sent to Fowey under the initial scheme.

The Council has been asked to make a preliminary allocation and to inform householders of the numbers allotted to them.

I am, therefore, to inform you that 2 child/children has/have been allotted to you.

It is expected that at some future date the Council will be notified that a further number of evacuees will be sent to Fowey, which may necessitate allotting another one or more evacuees to those houses where further accommodation has been offered and to those houses where no allotment has been made at this stage.

Yours faithfully,

J.W.Armstrong.

Chief Billeting Officer.

Letter to householders sent out by the local authorities in Cornwall, informing them 'you must take in evacuees'. (*Courtesy of Cornwall Council*)

Jean and Bern stayed in Reading until spring 1941, but they do not remember receiving love or comfort from their foster-mother. The only thing Jean really appreciated and wants to remember of her evacuation, was the freedom of the river and countryside which she enjoyed at the weekends.

Choosing a Billet

Vivienne Newell, then aged six and her sister Beryl, aged eight, were evacuated from Ilford to Ipswich in 1939.

'My sister and I were fostered by a couple who didn't want evacuees. They were told that the alternative was to billet soldiers, so they took us in. They were not unkind to us but didn't understand how to look after young girls.

'Beryl decided that we should move, so she and I walked across Ipswich to a house where some of our school friends were staying. The lady already had three girls of her own and two evacuees, but she allowed us to stay.

'There were five little girls in a double bed, with three at one end and two in the other! One of us left a doll behind at the previous billet, but their grown up son came and handed it over to us. I don't know if they were being kind or whether they didn't want us to have an excuse to go back to their home to collect the doll.'

Beryl Newell (left) and her sister Vivienne (right) were unhappy in their billet, so they found a new one for themselves. (*Courtesy of Derek Trayler*)

The girls remained in Ipswich until Beryl was diagnosed with scarlet fever. She and Vivienne were then sent home.

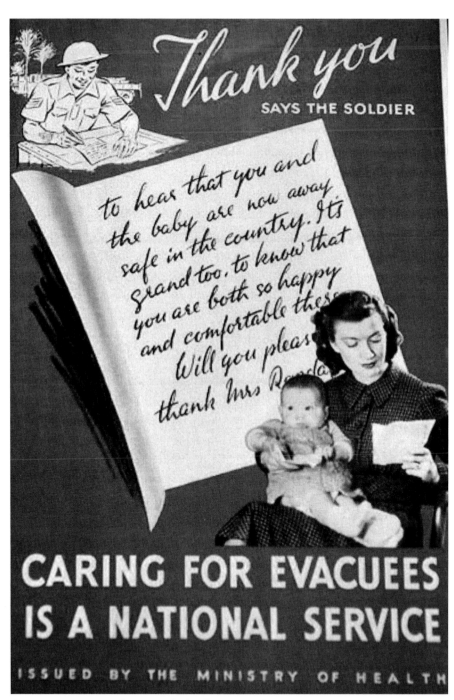

Government propaganda poster: 'Caring for evacuees is a national service'. (*Author's collection*)

An Air Raid at Sea

On the outbreak of war, 25-year-old Philip Godfray was Headmaster of Alderney School in the Channel Islands. Philip brought his pupils to safety in England, via Guernsey, in June 1940.

'The total length of the journey from Alderney was 60 hours with the delays. For the whole of this period the amazing spirit and faith of the children enabled them to respond to our guidance without a single whimper or word of complaint.

'At 5.30pm the ship parted from the historic quay. The National Anthem was struck up as the gap quickly widened between the silent crowds on shore and on board. It was, as any other music would have been, ridiculously inappropriate, but both sides, linked across the space by so many ties of parenthood and 'islandship' felt the need for a parting act together, and so that unique and mercifully short music filled the gap.

Philip Godfray, Headmaster of Alderney School, accompanied his pupils when they were evacuated to Cheshire. (*Courtesy of Anne Mauger*)

Channel Island evacuees in Manchester 1940. (*Courtesy of Bob Pearce*)

Philip's school was sent to Alderley Edge, in Cheshire. He arrived without essential paperwork, such as his teaching certificates or passport, as they had left at such short notice. He continued to teach in boys' boarding schools in England all his working life, returning to Alderney each year to see his family.

'I was standing just below the boat's bridge when the Blue Warning was brought down to me – an Air Raid at sea. I sent the boys down into the hold, while the others crowded under the shelter of the superstructure. Ten minutes crept by, half an hour. The gunner looked about him with a slightly disappointed expression. His rugged face seemed to say, 'Just let me have a shot at the blamed Nazis.'

'More time passed. We began to nibble the sandwiches – this frugal meal broke the spell. Ninety minutes. Suddenly the transmitter buzzed and spluttered into welcome staccato. It was over. And then, to the delighted eyes of our boys and girls, came the cliffs, the long lanes of ships, the docks, the trains, each to be explained, each part of the blessed wonder – of England.'

The Last to be Chosen

Eight-year-old Barry Fletcher was evacuated from Station Road School in Witton, near Birmingham, to Feckenham in Worcestershire in 1939

'I sat on the left hand side of the village hall, facing anxious children on the bench opposite, some crying, but most wide-eyed, tired and wishing they were back at home. I found myself next to a boy nearly two years older and gradually became aware of strangers arriving, pointing at children, usually the girls, and within a few minutes the child and adults disappeared out of the door.

'This process continued until only a handful of children remained. I spoke to the older boy sitting next to me. Harry was nearly ten years old, two classes above me at Station Road School, and not known to me before this unexpected event.

Barry Fletcher (centre, seated) with friends in the garden of 41 High Street, where he lived with the Spencer family. (*Courtesy of Barry Fletcher*)

'A teacher reassured Harry and I that someone would soon arrive and a home found for us. A further long wait before an elderly couple entered the hall. I sensed immediately that this was a reluctant act of kindness on their part, dutifully carried out to provide a temporary home for two very tired, lonely, hungry boys. We followed this couple, later known to us as Mr and Mrs Davis, back to their homely cottage in Droitwich Road, with a rear garden and chickens.

'They were really kind but it was more than they could cope with, and three months later we moved to the home of the Spencer family to stay with other evacuees and our teacher, Miss Barker. On several occasions Mum was given a lift to see me in Feckenham by a kind young man called Mr Hunt, who lived in Romsley.'

Barry returned home in 1941 with a mixture of childhood memories, after 18 months as an evacuee. In the 1990s he was fortunate enough to find Mr Hunt in Romsley, who remembered the former 'little evacuee' very well. Barry was able to thank him for his kindness all those years ago.

At War – with Porridge

Isobel Wotherspoon, then aged four, was evacuated from Clydebank to Girvan, Ayrshire, in September 1939.

'My mother took me, my brothers, Jim and Stewart, and my cousin to an aunt's house in the seaside town of Girvan. My mother and my cousin's mother took turns caring for us. On the morning that Mr Chamberlain's voice came over the radio to declare war, I was looking through a rain-swept window, wishing I could play at the seaside! War, to a four-year-old meant nothing.

'When my aunt was with us she insisted that I eat porridge before we left for school. I could not, and still cannot, bear even the smell of this food, so it was the one thing my mother did not insist on me eating. My brothers were

Isobel Wotherspoon, pictured with her mother and brothers, during her second evacuation to Girvan in 1941. (*Courtesy of Isobel Muir, née Wotherspoon*)

not too happy that most days they were late for school having to wait for me to finish my porridge!

'School was wonderful; a lovely stout, elderly teacher who cared for her group of infants in a large room, with a lovely warm enclosed fire in its centre. After six weeks we went home. On 14 March 1941 our whole family was evacuated to Girvan again, the day after Clydebank had its first visit from the Luftwaffe. We lived in an aunt's house for 18 months, with my father spending weekends with us, as the Singer factory where he worked, was back to production within a week of the Blitz.'

Isobel enjoyed her second stay in Girvan, as she was allowed to wander with her friends to the seashore or park and climb the nearby, bluebell-clad hills. She also discovered that people spoke with different accents and that some, such as the fisher folk from Aberdeenshire, were difficult to understand.

The 'Child Spy'

Glynis Wozniak's father, Joseph, fled a prisoner of war camp in Germany to Scotland in 1941, when he was just 12 years old.

'When Germany invaded the Ukraine, my father, Joseph Wozniak and his family were forcibly evacuated to Germany to undertake manual labour. One evening, he was cycling back from seeing a friend when he was accosted by two German soldiers, who accused him of being a 'child spy'. He was taken to Cornberg Prisoner of War Camp.

Joseph Wozniak with his wife and children, before Glynis and her twin brother were born. (*Courtesy of Glynis Wozniak*)

'One day he saw men being loaded onto a lorry and, without knowing where they were going, he sneaked into the lorry and joined them. They turned out to be Polish men who were being relocated to the UK. However, during the journey, Joseph was discovered amongst the men and removed from the lorry.

'Joseph managed to make his way to England and was sent to a prisoner of war camp, Deer Park, at Monymusk in Aberdeenshire. The camp had originally been named 'People's Displacement Camp number 111' and housed displaced eastern Europeans. By the time Joseph arrived, it had been converted into a prisoner of war camp for 17,000 men. Many prisoners worked on local farms and my father was taught to speak English by a local couple, George and Marjorie Pirie.'

After his release, Joseph became a barber in Torry, Aberdeen, and a favourite of the Aberdeen football team. Sadly, after only eight years of marriage, Joseph and his twin sons drowned during a fishing accident. Glynis spent 20 years tracing her father's family in the Ukraine. They told her that, for the rest of his life, Joseph's brother had told everyone, 'I have a brother and will one day meet him again'.

Studying Algebra and Scrumping for Pears

Doreen Moss, then aged nine, was evacuated with Westleigh Junior School, Leigh-on-Sea, Essex to Kniveton, near Ashbourne, Derbyshire in September 1939.

'Twelve children, mostly brothers and sisters, were gathered in the school hall where prospective foster parents assembled. I had a label round my neck saying 'brother to follow, has chicken pox'. This meant I was left till last and went home with Muriel and her mother. Unfortunately, next morning Muriel was found to have German measles. I was immediately taken to a children's home in Hartington, some distance away. Imagine the shock, horror of a child, the first time away from home.

'On the third day our headmaster found me and somehow, my mother and brother appeared. She was asked to stay in the village to keep an eye on the

Doreen Moss (front row, second from the right) pictured with her school friends in Derbyshire. (*Courtesy of Doreen Sporle (Née Moss)*)

evacuees and this she did. I passed my scholarship and moved to Westcliff High School in Chapel-en-le-Frith. For six weeks I lived happily with two sisters, the Misses Wright. My last meal was memorable for all the wrong reasons, tripe and onions, in a thick white sauce. I had never heard of tripe before and was quite unable to eat it!

'Another move was to Eaves Hall, which was used as the senior school. I was happy there and remember scrumping enough pears from the tree to give to everyone in my class for lunch, with permission of course. I also remember the drama of not understanding one word of algebra, until something suddenly clicked a couple of days before the exam – and I gained 92 per cent!

'During the long school holidays, I visited my mother and younger brother in Shirley, where they were billeted with the Redshaw family.'

Westcliff High School returned home in October 1942. In later life, despite the hardships of the war, Doreen's mother reached the grand old age of 108.

An Unlikely Pair

Joseph Parry, then aged 11, was evacuated with St Monica's Catholic Primary School, Bootle, to Southport in September 1939.

'One day we were told "Bring your gas masks into school with you tomorrow, and some clothes, because you're going on holiday!" They queued us up outside the school and we walked to Ford Station, two miles away. We all piled onto the waiting train and I thought 'Where are we all going?' The teachers had told us we were headed to Southport, further up the coast, and far from the bombs that would soon rain down on Bootle. In Southport we were loaded onto a bus to travel to Norwood Road School.

Ruined by wartime bombing, St Luke's Church, Liverpool, now serves as a memorial to those who died during the Mersyside Blitz. (*Courtesy of Neil Holmes*)

Joseph Parry survived the Merseyside Blitz and later served in the Merchant Navy, when this picture was taken. (*Courtesy of Becky Williams*)

'The Norwood Road children had been given half a day off to allow the Bootle children to go into the school hall to be billeted. I was sitting with our Phil, who had his arm in plaster of Paris after falling off a wall back in Park Street. When people came in to choose their evacuees, I think they saw Phil's arm and thought 'We'll have to take him to hospital all the time!'

'Luckily kindly Mrs Rimmer took us home to live with her husband and their son John, but not before we were given a parcel each containing a tin of corned beef, two bars of York chocolate and a tin of condensed milk.'

Joseph later rejoined his family, who had moved to Wigan where his father had found work. Later they moved back to Bootle, where they lived through the worst of the bombing raids. By the end of the Merseyside Blitz, as it was known, 4,000 people had died. Joseph passed away in October 2013.

Birthday at War

Six-year-old Ralph Risk from Pollokshields was evacuated with Kelvinside Academy, Glasgow to the Isle of Arran on 2 September 1939.

'I do not remember the train journey from Hampden Park to Ardrossan, nor the ferry trip on the SS *Duchess of Hamilton* across to Brodick. This is surprising, as my father was President of Queen's Park Football Club! However, I remember being very upset that evening, and was comforted by Mrs Young, the junior school teacher.

'The following day was fateful for Britain but also for me. It was my seventh birthday and at 11am it was announced on the radio that Britain was at war with Germany. I had received a present of a Dinky truck, complete with a wind-up barrage balloon, and was very upset when the older boys used the balloon as a football and damaged it beyond repair.

'As winter approached, Dougrie Lodge was too remote and inadequately heated, so we moved to the Royal Hotel, Tyndrum. Prior to departure,

Ralph Risk (pictured on the front row, rubbing his eyes) with Kelvinside Academy at Dougrie Lodge, Isle of Arran. (*Courtesy of Kelvinside Academy*)

Mrs Young phoned the navy to report a submarine sighting off Arran, to be told, "Don't be so bloody silly, madam, we do not have one in that area!" We departed Arran on Friday 24 November on the SS *Dalriada* and I have a memory of a warship coming up alongside us and hailing, "We got it!", meaning a German submarine.

'Later we moved to the Tarbet Hotel and one day visited Tarbet Station to see King George VI and Queen Elizabeth arrive to visit Arrochar submarine base. We noticed a chocolate machine and one boy put a penny in and it dispensed a chocolate bar – the machine had lain untouched since the outbreak of war. Everyone scrambled to empty the machine with their pennies, but I did not have a penny and ended up without chocolate!'

In January 1944 Ralph and the other boys returned to their homes in Glasgow and schooling at Kelvinside Academy recommenced.

Separated from Siblings

Peter Campbell, then aged six, was evacuated from Folkestone to Merthyr Tydfil, South Wales, in May 1940.

'People were lining the street right to the top, waving flags and cheering, trying to make us welcome. Halfway up the hill the string on my parcel came off and I dropped everything all over the street. Some kind ladies ran forward, wrapped them up again and carried my parcel to the mission hall. They told me and my brother and sisters that we would not be able to stay together. I was to stay with my sister Pat, but my sister Ivy would be on her own, as would Gordon and Terry. Soon a couple came to us to take us to their home – a Mr and Mrs Evans.

'The first night was very strange. I did not sleep very well, and wanted to be back home with my Mum and Dad. Pat said the war would not last very long, we would soon be home again. We went to St Illtyd's School and everybody there thought we were funny because we did not talk like them, but they were nice to us.

'After a couple of weeks we realised that things were not right – Mr and Mrs Evans were cruel to us. We were told not to come home till late; sometimes we went to school without breakfast. I cried a lot and told my teacher that I wanted to go home. Pat told her teacher they were cruel to us. The next day we moved in with Mr and Mrs Mahoney, who were very nice and made us welcome with good food, warm and comfortable beds. They wrote to our parents to tell them we were OK.'

When Peter and Pat returned home two years later, they couldn't help thinking about Mr and Mrs Mahoney, who had looked after them so well, and the school friends they had left behind.

Pat Campbell (left) and her brother Peter (right) were badly treated in their first billet in Merthyr Tydfil. (*Courtesy of Peter Campbell*)

Refuge in Rochdale

Leonard Cox fled Jersey with his wife Alyce and their four younger children and settled in Rochdale, Lancashire, in June 1940.

The Garfath Cox family encountered a very different world when they were evacuated from Jersey to Rochdale in 1940. (*Courtesy of Audrey Wilson*)

'At the harbour our sons were put onto a cargo boat, but the rest of us could not find room on any ship. I returned to the boys' boat, asking "Will you please just take my wife and daughters? I'm too old" The man on the gangway agreed, then as he saw our tearful farewells, said "Oh come on, old man, get on!"

'We settled down on the hatch-cover of a hold as the sun was setting on a calm sea, and after an uneventful night, we berthed at Weymouth. We were asked if we had relatives or friends who could accommodate us in the UK, but like us, the majority had nowhere to go and very little money.'

Leonard's son Graeme recalls: 'We boarded a train and soon realised that we were heading north. The following morning we pulled into a railway station where I managed to read a painted-out sign 'Rochdale'. I had never heard of the place, but someone mentioned that it was where Gracie Fields came from. This trivial bit of information was strangely comforting. I had seen Gracie Fields in films and felt that if they were like her in Rochdale we would be all right. We were taken to a large empty house where women and girls were placed in some rooms and men and boys in others and my father was put in charge of the group.

'Our reception by the local people was basic but wonderful because they were so welcoming. However the sight of tall chimneys smoking day and night and the clatter of clogs on cobbled streets was a complete contrast to the island we had left.'

Sadly, Alyce died in Rochdale in October 1943, which was a devastating blow for the family, and they decided to remain in England after the war.

Evacuee Under Arrest

John Honeybone, then aged eight, was evacuated with his mother and sisters from Barnet to Portland, Dorset in 1944.

'We left because of the doodlebugs; my friend was killed and our house was hit. Mum said "We have lost our roof, so we are going." My Dad was in the army. We were sent to two different billets but we were not happy there. We then went to stay with Mum's brother who lived on a council estate right next to Portland dockyard. Tunnels next to the dockyard were used as ammunition dumps, so if a bomb had hit them, that would have been the end of Portland! My parents were constantly worrying about this.

'There were three bedrooms, so it was overcrowded with Uncle Arthur, Auntie Ada and their three grown-up children, plus me, Mum, and my sisters. They were a very down-to-earth family and kind to us. Aunt Ada used to walk round with an uncut loaf of bread under her arm and ask "Are you hungry duck?" and if we said "Yes" she would cut us a slice of bread and spread it with butter.

'We attended school but the local children were unfriendly. Our accents stood out and we were called 'incomers'. I really wanted to see the big ships in the dockyard, so one day I walked to the gates, there was no one on guard duty so I walked in. Suddenly blue lights were flashing and I was arrested! It was even mentioned in the local newspaper!'

John found it strange when he returned to Barnet in 1945. Their house was still being repaired and John was later disappointed because he failed his Eleven Plus examination. He believes that this was because of the disruption to his education through attending different schools with different methods of teaching.

John wishes to dedicate his story to his mother, Dorothy.

John Honeybone (far right) with his parents and sister Sylvia, a few years before the evacuation. (*Courtesy of John Honeybone*)

Bombs and Bugs

Lourdes Galliano, then aged 12, was evacuated from Gibraltar to London, in July 1940.

'My mother, my two sisters and I arrived in London and were taken to the Empress Hall in Earl's Court, a skating rink that had been converted into an evacuee reception centre. The rows of tiered seats in the hall had been closed and folding camp beds had been jammed into the gaps – there were 750 of us!

'We were very tired but, as we lay on our camp beds we could see that the domed ceiling was entirely made of glass. Not very reassuring had we known what was to come! The next morning there was no sign of our luggage but ladies from the Women's Voluntary Service had set up long tables full of second-hand clothes and underwear. We also received a medical and a hot bath.

'The conditions were impossible, as there were always queues for the toilets and the washbasins and they both deteriorated progressively. I remember one morning, carrying my soap and towel to a basin, and just before setting them down, noticing that the bar of soap already there seemed to move by itself. I looked closely and sure enough it was so covered in lice that it actually moved!

'One night the lights had just been turned down when we heard the loud wail of the air raid warning. Everyone jumped out of bed, but we didn't know where to turn with this menacing glass dome above us. We were directed to a shelter outside and a couple of hours later we crawled gratefully back to our folding camp beds, only to find most of them covered in glass from the panes which had fallen in during the bombing.'

Lourdes' family were later moved into a hotel in Kensington. In July 1944 they were sent to Warbleshinny Camp in Londonderry, where they lived in very basic conditions in Nissan huts. They returned to Gibraltar in January 1945.

Lourdes Galliano was evacuated from Gibraltar in 1940, right into the heart of the London Blitz. (*Courtesy of Lourdes Galliano*)

An Older Evacuee

Dorothy Reynolds, then aged 16, was evacuated with Westcliff High School for Girls, Westcliff on Sea, Essex, to Derbyshire in June 1940.

'I was in the Lower Sixth Form at school when the Government announced plans to evacuate children from the coastal areas, so we went by train to Chapel-en-le Frith Station, with one piece of luggage, lunch and a gas mask. We wore our winter uniform and it was a very hot day. On arrival we were welcomed with tea and sandwiches in the Constitution Hall, then our heads and throats were inspected by nurses.

'Some girls were found billets in Chapel, whilst others went to Chinley. Here we saw the notice 'Please will you come to the Women's Institute at 6pm to offer these poor children homes?' Again some were found billets, but I went with a small group to Buxworth, where Mrs Phillips and her daughter Ivy made Mary and me very welcome.

'They told us later they had been expecting small children and were prepared to bath them and tuck them up in bed, they had not reckoned to receive two large 16-year-olds. Their home was a small house at the end of a terrace, 'Brookside'. It had a living room with a cooking range, a kitchen, two bedrooms, no bathroom and an outside lavatory. They were very kind people.'

SOUTHEND-ON-SEA EDUCATION COMMITTEE.
EDUCATION OFFICE, WARRIOR SQUARE, SOUTHEND-ON-SEA.

29th May, 1940.

THE GOVERNMENT'S EVACUATION SCHEME.

The assembly point for your
child *Dorothy   Reynolds*
is *Westcliff High School for Girls*
The party number is *Southend 46*

Dorothy Reynolds' evacuation notice. (*Courtesy of Dorothy Walsh née Reynolds*)

Dorothy Reynolds considers herself to have been very lucky in her experiences as an evacuee in Derbyshire. (*Courtesy of Dorothy Walsh née Reynolds*)

Dorothy kept in touch with the Phillips family for some years, later visiting Ivy in Whaley Bridge, where her husband had an antiques shop.

Taking the Kindertransport to Safety in Scotland

Kurt Gutmann, then aged 12, escaped from Nazi Germany to Annan, Scotland, in June 1939

Kurt Gutmann (right) was evacuated from Germany to the Chalmers family in Scotland, and still visits George Chalmers (left) every year. (*Courtesy of Rod Edgar, Dumfriesshire Newspapers Group*)

'My family are German Jews and our father died when I was very young. I remember the Nazis in the street, the posters saying 'The Jews are our misfortune', and I was beaten up at school for being 'dirty'. One day my uncle was thrown out of a second floor window and died instantaneously.

'I was sent to the UK for safety with thousands of other Jewish children. My mother put my brother and I on a train at Mulheim Station and kissed us goodbye. I didn't realise it at the time, but I would never see her again.

'My brother and I were sent to Annan and were very fortunate to be taken into the home of James and Florence Chalmers. I had never really known my own father, and Mr Chalmers treated me as his own son. For the first time in my life, I was able to be a child, to play with young George Chalmers, to

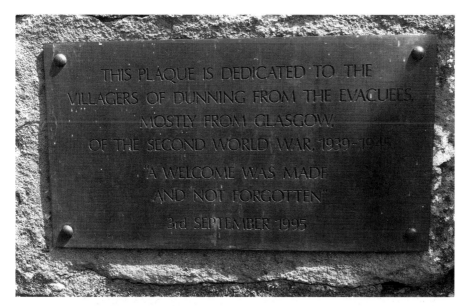

This plaque in Dunning, Scotland, pays tribute to those who cared for evacuees from Glasgow and, like Kurt, from much further afield. (*Courtesy of Spot On Locations*)

go the cinema on a Saturday and eat fish and chips. I could even swim at Waterfoot without being accused of 'dirtying the waters'. For the first time, I was a real human being.

'In 1942 I joined the war effort in Glasgow, and in 1944 I enlisted into the Black Watch. My brother remained in Scotland, but in 1948 I returned home to help rebuild a Nazi-free Germany.'

When Kurt returned to Germany, he tried to find his mother and older brother. They had both died in a concentration camp in Sobibor, Poland. In 2009 he testified against Jon Demjanjuk, who was accused of participating in the murder of 27,000 people at Sobibor. Kurt returns to Annan every year to visit George Chalmers.

Well Looked After

Nine-year-old Gwen Woodhatch was evacuated with her sister Audrey, aged five, from Sydenham, London, to Bideford, Devon, in June 1940.

Gwen Burchell (left) and her sister Audrey (far right) with Mr and Mrs Shute, who provided them with a loving home in Bideford. (*Courtesy of Bideford Heritage,* www. bidefordheritage.co.uk)

'We were taken together, which was fortunate, by 'Auntie and Uncle Shute'. Nice people and a nice house. On our first Christmas a large cardboard box arrived from London and we eagerly opened it in bed. Matching jumpers together with pixie hoods, all knitted by Mum. Cross and chain for each of us together with other goodies. Wonderful!

'After 18 months we were taken from Elm Grove as 'Uncle Shute' had unfortunately died and 'Auntie' needed to take adult lodgers into her home to earn more money. We moved into a hostel until a second billet could be found for us. Our new guardian was a Miss Gabriel, who lived in Barnstaple Street opposite the wharf. She was about 60 years old, very prim and proper, stone deaf, and wore long skirts, with her hair tied back into a bun. She looked after us well. We used to love the laverbread she fried up for breakfast – a seaweed which is a Welsh traditional dish, but also found in the West Country.

'We loved the visits from Mum and Aunt Charlotte, who used to take us for days out to Instow, Westward Ho and Clovelly. Dad was unable to visit on a regular basis because he was a railway signalman at the Crystal Palace, a very essential service at the time.'

Even 1940s advertising featured evacuees, like this one from Bisto. (*Author's collection*)

Due to the long separation from their parents, in 1943 Gwen became depressed and the doctor advised that the girls return home for fear of a nervous breakdown. After the war they stayed in touch with 'Auntie Shute' and visited her several times before she died.

Joining the Crocodile

Derek Trayler, then aged seven, was evacuated, by sea, from Dagenham, Essex, to Norfolk in September 1939.

'My brother and I joined the procession and started to move up the bridge to the station at the top. This is about 100 yards and normally takes a few minutes, but we were moving very slowly. It was still dark at the bottom but dawn was breaking by the time we got half-way. It was completely light by the time we got to the top and could see the other side.

Derek Trayer (left) with Doreen Keeler and his brother John (back) were well cared for by Mr and Mrs Keeler. (*Courtesy of Derek Trayler*)

'What we saw then was the most amazing sight and one I hope we never see again. From the station and all the way down Valance Avenue was a complete line of young children going on into the distance. Out of each side turning there were more crocodiles of children emerging. Each one was adding to the line, which by now was spreading half-way across Dagenham.

'After walking five miles, we arrived at Dagenham Docks. Facing us were three paddle steamers, which took Londoners on excursions to Southend and Margate. On deck we were told to go on round to the other side, where we crossed a long gangplank to the next ship. We hung on the rail without moving all the way down the Thames and up the East Coast, until we turned in to Yarmouth. The couple, Mr and Mrs Keeler, who took us in had a six-year-old daughter, Doreen, and gave up their own bedroom for us. They treated us very well, with the same loving care that my parents would have done for their children, if the roles had been reversed.'

After the war Derek and his brother went back on separate occasions to see Mr and Mrs Keeler and Doreen visited them too. However, when Dr Beeching closed their railway line in the 1960s, it become more difficult for them to meet.

London evacuees arrive in Wolverhampton during 1944. (*Courtesy of the* Wolverhampton Express and Star)

Cinema Trips and Bags of Chips

John Martin, then aged seven, was evacuated from Dagenham to Burnley, Lancashire, in 1943

'I had a very nice place to live with Mr and Mrs Bromley at 5 Lawn Street, in Colne, near Burnley. They did not have any children of their own, so I was looked after very well. I called them Uncle Bill and Auntie Peg, and they had a nice clean house next to a coal mine.

'After six months Mrs Bromley became ill so I had to go to another family. This time it wasn't so good. The house was shoddy and not clean; they had no idea how to look after children. My room was the junk room in the attic, full of old stuff they had no use for. The bed was never made and the room was never cleaned the whole time I was there.

'I had to prepare my own food, which was usually toast and jam, sometimes some bacon or a pork chop. The nearest thing to a cooked meal was chips and peas from the chip shop. Even so, I was never unhappy. I had lots of friends and the big weekly treat was going to the cinema on a Thursday night. We couldn't get sweets, so we took in a bag of chopped carrots and swede to munch during the film. I didn't see my parents whilst I was away, but had letters and presents for Christmas and birthdays.'

When John returned home, his mother didn't recognise him as he had turned into a 'dirty, scruffy street urchin'. She also had trouble understanding him as he had developed a north country accent. She put him in the bath, threw away his scruffy clothes and cooked him a proper meal.

John Martin, pictured here after joining the navy, aged 15, had a very mixed experience as an evacuee in Burnley during the war. (*Courtesy of John Martin*)

'I Don't Want to Go Home'

Richard Singleton, then aged 10, was evacuated from Liverpool to Bronant, near Aberystwyth in 1940.

'My brother Ron and I were cared for by Elizabeth (Liz) and Moses Morgan, at Tancwarel Farm, and we were so very happy living there. Farm life was good, summer or winter. In winter Ron, Aunty and I played dominoes in front of a roaring peat fire. In spring, lambs were being born, hens sitting on the eggs, so no school – life was great.

'We grew very close to Aunty Liz because she looked after us, and if she went anywhere, we would be right behind her. If one of us got hurt she would give us a hug and say, "Come here my love" (in Welsh). Our mother would never have said that, it would be, "Don't be a cry baby."

'After some time, our Mam arrived at the farm, to take us home. I told her I didn't want to go home. Ron, Aunty and I were crying, so in the end she let me stay and said she would be back for me. I was still crying when Ron left, and I really missed him. When Mam came to visit again about six months later, it was just like the last time, crying and not wanting to go. Aunty gave me a pen and pencil set, plus the New Testament that she had given me when we first arrived.

'Mum wanted me home because I was coming to the age of leaving school, 14. I cannot remember leaving – I was too upset to think of never seeing Aunty, Moses and everything that I loved on the farm.'

Richard next saw Aunty Liz when he took his family on holiday to Wales in the 1960s. His one regret is that he never told her that he loved her for giving him and Ron a wonderful life while they were under her care.

Richard Singleton (centre, front) with members of his family and his 'foster mother' Miss Liza Morgan. (*Courtesy of Richard Singleton*)

A Seaside Stay

Londoner, Norton Myhill, then aged nine, was evacuated with his school to Dorset in September 1939.

'I was firstly evacuated to Sturminster Newton, but when I moved up to secondary school, I had to go to Kingston in South Dorset. I arrived there with my guardians from North Dorset and they introduced themselves to my new guardians. The lady smiled at me with a big welcoming grin; I fell in love with her then and it lasted a lifetime.

'The next two years with Auntie Hilda, Uncle Ern and their son Colin were the some of the most memorable of my life. Auntie would decide on a picnic and we would all pitch in cleaning the house, making sandwiches and head off to the beach at the drop of a hat. The villagers and evacuees got along great and I joined the choir.

'There was a Commando unit stationed in the village and early one morning the vicar threw stones at my bedroom window. He was rounding up the choir for a special service for the Commandos going on a mission. They never came back. It was the raid on Dieppe.

'In 1943 the number of evacuees declined to about a dozen, with only one teacher. The authorities decided to close the school, so Father got me into a partially state-supported school, Archbishop Tenison's. It had been evacuated to Earley near Reading, Berkshire. I went there and flourished, finishing up first in my class, despite skipping a year to make up for my late arrival.'

In the summer of 1944 a Doodlebug hit an office on the opposite side of the road to Norton's family's apartment. All the doors and windows were blown apart, but his parents were not hurt. Norton stayed in touch with Auntie Hilda until her death.

Norton Myhill (left) with his foster father Uncle Ern and foster brother Colin. (*Courtesy of Norton Myhill*)

Bless my life! what's this I see?
If it isn't a little EVACUEE
Don't be afraid
when it's dark at night
They simply can't put out my light.

Idyllic postcards like this one were produced for evacuees to send to their parents. (*Author's collection*)

Chapter Two

A Different World:
Adjusting to Life Away from Home

The stories in this chapter come from evacuees who found themselves embarking on a new life overnight. City children were sent from highly populated, heavily built-up areas to quiet villages in the countryside. Some, accustomed to homes with 'all mod cons', found themselves in cottages where there was no running water, or gas and electricity.

Equally, children from working class houses were evacuated to middle and upper class homes, and some were surprised to find themselves now waited on by servants. One evacuee recalled, 'During the war I lived in luxury but in 1945 had to return to reality'. As Jean Burton points out in her story, some children were evacuated to industrial areas which were in fact at far greater risk of bombing than those they had left behind.

Evacuation of Gateshead schoolchildren in 1939. (*Courtesy of Gateshead Libraries*)

There were new dialects and accents to absorb and understand, sometimes new languages to learn. Whole schools were evacuated and uprooted to unfamiliar environments with their teachers, and allowances were rarely made for religious or cultural differences.

Evacuated to a Mansion

Doreen Acton (née Mason), then aged 17, was evacuated with Westcliff High School for Girls, Westcliff on Sea, Essex, to Chapel-en-le-Frith, Derbyshire, in June 1940.

'The local people began to choose us, which was a bit like a slave auction! Four of us upper sixth formers were driven off in a large car with a chauffeur to an impressive mansion, Bowden Hall, just outside Chapel-en-le-Frith. Our eyes opened wide as we were greeted by Mr Lauder, a friendly looking elderly gentleman, who shook our hands. Freda and Beryl were directed to bedrooms in the mansion, whilst Audrey and I were taken to the chauffeur's cottage. We looked with dismay at the double bed we were to share, so we removed the bolster and placed it between us. We did not know then

Doreen Mason with her Uncle Charlie in 1935. Five years later, Doreen was evacuated to a mansion in Derbyshire. (*Courtesy of Doreen Acton, née Mason*)

that the chauffeur and his wife had given up their bed for us.

'We returned to the mansion and were introduced to a visitor, Sir William Clare-Lees, and tried to look as though we were accustomed to such company! Chrissie, the Scottish maid was a very good cook and there seemed to be no shortage of food as we were surrounded by farms. Mr Lauder took us on wonderful outings in the chauffeur-driven car.

'A few weeks later, Mrs Lauder returned home and I got the impression that she thought we had been allowed too much liberty, as we were consigned to the kitchen for meals. However, she soon realised we were quite house-trained and no threat to peace and order and treated us as kindly and generously as her husband.'

Westcliff High School pupils arrive at Chapel-en-le-Frith station, in Derbyshire June 1940.
(*Courtesy of Whaley Bridge Archives*)

When Doreen left school she did not gain a university scholarship, so went to work at the Bank of England. She later discovered that Mr Lauder had offered to pay her university fees, and, though immensely touched, she felt too awkward to pursue this offer. Thirty five years later she enrolled in the Open University to gain the degree that she missed out on in her youth.

The 'Witches' of Winster

Seven-year-old June Somekh from Manchester was evacuated with Cavendish Road Primary School to Winster in Derbyshire.

A street in Winster, pictured in 1960: June Somekh spent her evacuation in this village, billeted in the home of two 'witches'. (*Courtesy of John Williams*)

'My brother, sister and I ended up in a hut where there seemed to be hundreds of people milling around. We were each given a carrier bag and had to walk past a line of women who each put a can of food into it. Now came the 'allocation' of the children. I remember hearing, "Two girls, they'll do for Miss Smith." We didn't then know what had happened to our brother.

'We had left a large house in Manchester with modern facilities and were taken to a much smaller one with no electricity or running water. Miss Smith was somewhat older than my grandmother, but she was very kind and I grew to love her. However, the problem was a much larger lady who used to shout, "You licker newt, you kipper 'addock," at us. With hindsight I think she had Tourette's Syndrome, but we were terrified and thought we were staying with two witches. We decided that one of us should stay awake at all times. Needless to say, we soon dropped off.

'Our parents came to visit and I occasionally went home to Manchester. Father did not feel that the allowance was enough to feed us so he sent extra money, whilst mother sent parcels of goodies.'

No account was taken of religion or ethnicity when June was billeted. She came from an Orthodox Jewish home, but she was expected to attend Sunday School and her brother was billeted with a pork butcher!

Hoping for Daddy to Come Home

James Brown, then aged five, was evacuated from Liverpool to Hindley, Lancashire, with his mother Anne and his younger sisters, Emily and Rhona, in June 1942.

'We were evacuated when Mum discovered that our father was missing in action. She took us away from Liverpool for safety's sake. We arrived in Hindley, Wigan which was very rural compared to the terraced streets of Liverpool.

'We lived with a lovely lady, Mrs Lee, and her home was warm and welcoming with many rooms and plenty of open spaces externally. She was very kind to us, but my mother's most vivid memory is that we were persuaded to drink a herbal drink that Mrs Lee mixed herself. It was most unpleasant but Mrs Lee claimed it lengthened your life!

'I attended the local school and struggled to mix with the local children at first, because their accents were difficult for me to understand. In our spare time we played board games, listened to the radio and played in a farmer's field at the rear of the house. We returned home shortly before the war ended because we learned, via a broadcast from the Vatican, that our father was alive but in an Italian prisoner of war camp.'

James found it difficult to adjust from life in Liverpool to life in Hindley, and he missed his father terribly. After the war, the family sent a Christmas card to Mrs Lee every year.

James Brown (right) was fortunate to be evacuated with his mother Anne and his sisters Emily (left) and Rhona (seated on Anne's knee). (*Courtesy of Mackenzie Brown*)

A Place of Greater Danger

Three-year-old Jean Burton was evacuated from her home in Dunfermline, Scotland, to Wolverhampton in the West Midlands.

'We lived near Rosyth Dockyard and, when war was declared, the dockyard was brought up to strength. My Mum, Petrina, became an assistant riveter, passing red hot rivets to the male welders to repair ships and submarines. Rosyth and the Forth Bridge were considered prime German targets, so the government ordered that local children should be evacuated. However, Mum refused to send my sister Margaret and I away.

'Each day was fraught with danger at the dockyard, and Mum faced hostility from some male colleagues. However, once they realised she could pull her weight, things became more tolerable and she made good friends. In 1940, bombings occurred around Rosyth, and Mum decided to send us to her family in Wolverhampton, believing it to be less of a target.

'My aunts Marjory, Barbara and Jean worked shifts at the Boulton Paul aircraft factory, but I spent most time with Barbara and some of her neighbours assumed that I was her own child. Wolverhampton was very different to Dunfermline, and I had to get used to the different accent and dialect. I missed my mum too, very badly.

'There were actually more bombing raids in Wolverhampton than at Rosyth. German maps found at the end of war showed that the Boulton Paul factory was a major target. It survived because of a dummy factory built two miles to the north, which was bombed three times by the Germans!'

Jean returned to Dunfermline after a few years in Wolverhampton. She still keeps in regular touch with her aunt Barbara.

Jean Burton (pictured as a baby) was sent to Wolverhampton by her mother Petrina. (*Courtesy of Jean Hoban, née Burton*)

The Luxury of an 'Inside Bathroom'

In September 1939, during the first wave of evacuations, Ethel Henson, then aged 13, was evacuated from Nottingham to Mansfield.

Ethel Henson in later life: Ethel formed a lasting bond with Mrs Carlin, her foster mother. (*Courtesy of Ethel Basford, née Henson*)

'My sister and I were evacuated with Trent Bridge School to Billthorpe in Mansfield. Ladies and gentlemen came along to choose us and, because people only wanted one child, my sister and I went to live with different families.

'I was lucky as I was chosen by a lovely couple, Mr and Mrs Carlin – he was a miner at Billthorpe Mine. They had no children but had a lovely house, which was very posh compared to my home in Trent Bridge. What seemed a real luxury was having a bathroom inside the house and I had my own bedroom, too. They looked after me really well and Mrs Carlin took me into Mansfield to buy me new clothes.

'We saw my own family quite a bit, because Mum visited as often as she could. Dad was in the Forces but he was based at a camp close to Trent Bridge, so my Mum, sister and I could visit him. One day Mum came to collect me and took me home for good – I had to start work, as she needed the money. I visited the Carlins after the war, and on one occasion there was no one home. A neighbour told me that Mrs Carlin was at the hairdresser's and when I got there, she was really pleased to see me, and I had my hair done too!'

The photograph is the only one taken of Ethel when she was younger. She lost all her family papers and childhood photographs in the floods of 1947.

A Different Life

Jim Marshall, then aged nine, was evacuated from Rochford, Kent, to Bream, Gloucestershire in September 1939.

At Priors Lodge, Jim Marshall and his brother Dick spent the war years in luxury. (*Courtesy of Jim Marshall*)

'My brother Dick and I were very lucky as we were chosen, along with five other boys, by Mrs Percival, who lived at a huge manor house, Priors Lodge. The following morning, we looked out of the window with disbelief to see a huge long drive, which seemed to disappear for miles into the distance!

'Priors Lodge was enormous, with around 40 acres of grounds, a trout lake, and tennis courts. There was a cook, two housemaids, a gardener and a woodsman. Major and Mrs Percival's sons had been evacuated to Canada, so it was nice for them to have boys in the house, and they took a real interest in our welfare and education.

'At first we had a bedroom each, but they removed the table from the billiard room, and put seven beds in there so that were all together. The Major was a Conservative but she was staunch Labour, so at dinner, they would sit at opposite ends of the table and have the occasional argument over politics.

'I only saw Mum once during the war, but we did exchange letters. Our house was right across the road from Southend Airport, where Spitfires were taking off and landing, so Mum and Dad didn't get much sleep during the war! I was with the Percivals until the war ended, and when their sons returned from Canada.'

When Jim returned home, he found it very difficult. He was 14 years old and Rochford was now very unfamiliar, as were his parents. His evacuation had been a life-changing experience, as Jim had enjoyed a privileged lifestyle, but in 1945 he had to return home to reality. He stayed in touch with the Percivals until they passed away, and recently visited Priors Lodge, which, he says hasn't changed much since his years there.

From Tearaway to Country Boy

William (Bill) Flynn, then aged six, was evacuated with his sisters Tessie and Ann from St Anthony's Roman Catholic School in Liverpool to Pitchford, Shrewsbury, in September 1939.

'It was a real wrench for me to leave my large family and my home, and the journey to Pitchford was an arduous one. We arrived at a manor house, then were all allocated to Mr and Mrs Jones in a farm cottage. They were kind and generous people and would kiss and cuddle us before bedtime, unlike our father who was not very tactile. In Liverpool I had been a bit of a tearaway, always up to mischief, but in Pitchford this kind of behaviour gradually stopped.

'The rural setting of Shrewsbury could not have been more different to our rough and tumble working class area in Liverpool. I made friends at the local school but was lucky to have a friend from Liverpool living nearby, Reggie Lucy. We were the same age and spent every spare moment together. On one occasion we saw a plane crash into a nearby field and found some bullets close to where the plane had landed. My sister Tessie, Reggie and I would frequently roam around the fields to observe the wildlife and unusual sights.'

Bill felt that his experience in Pitchford shaped his future life, as he was always interested in wildlife and gardening. He stayed in touch with the Jones family after the war.

During their evacuation, Bill Flynn (left) and his sister Tessie (centre) were reunited with a friend from home, Reggie Lucy (right). (*Courtesy of Mackenzie Brown*)

A Make-Shift Boarding School

Gordon Lancaster, then aged 13, was evacuated with Derby Grammar School to Amber Valley Camp, near Ashover, in 1940.

Amber Valley Camp, where Gordon Lancaster spent three years as an evacuee with Derby Grammar School. (*Courtesy of Derbyshire Times*)

'Firstly, we went to Overton Hall, near Ashover, although some boys were billeted in the village as there were so many of us. I had just recovered from scarlet fever and had to obtain a medical certificate to show that I was clear of infection. In June 1940 we moved to a large camp at Amber Valley, so all the boys could be together. The camp contained newly built wooden huts, a big dining hall, assembly hall, dormitories and a tuck shop. I rather liked it there and I went home during school holidays.

'The winter of 1940 was very bad and some of us got stuck in very deep snow, at the top of a hill between Ashover and Overton Hall. A postman saw us there and told those at the Hall where we were. Some of our teachers came out to us and we got into trouble because we had been told to walk round by Milltown, rather than climb the steep hill.'

After three years, Gordon left Amber Valley Camp to work on the railways. A reunion is organised by the former evacuees each year to mark the move from Overton Hall to Amber Valley camp. It takes place at Ogston sailing club, which was the camp's dining room and is now the only remaining part of the camp.

First Time in the Countryside

Sylvia Rigley, then aged eight, was evacuated from Liverpool to Chirk, North Wales, in September 1939.

Sylvia Rigley attended Chirk Girls School when she was evacuated to North Wales. (*Author's collection*)

'We were packed off with our belongings in rucksacks and packed lunches, with some teachers in charge. A lot of my friends and their parents were in tears, but to me it was just a great adventure. In Chirk we were assigned to different families and I had a good home and a bedroom to myself for the first time.

'There wasn't enough room in the school for us at first, so we just did half-days and had lovely walks with our teachers. We also had the use of a big house where we sat around a coal fire and read, did handicrafts and learned to knit. It was the first time most of us had been to the countryside. I loved it, feeding the ducks on the canal, picking blackberries and chestnuts. After six months I returned to Liverpool, homesick.'

Sylvia was later evacuated to a village in Cheshire and she returned to Liverpool in 1941.

Evacuated Back Home

Gerry Mullan, then aged six, was evacuated from Belfast, Northern Ireland, to County Tyrone in 1941.

'We went to Fintona, where we had lived three or four years earlier. I felt excited and apprehensive, because I wasn't sure what it was going to be like to live in someone else's house. My brother Joe and I were looked after by a woman called Mrs Martin, an old friend of my mother. She was good, but very strict.

'Mother came with us, but she and my younger brothers were housed four or five miles away. We saw her once a week but it was a bit heart-rending. I renewed acquaintances with some of the children I had known years earlier, which was good, but although Mrs Martin was very kind I remember never being really sure whether I was happy or not. We were very hard-up in Tyrone, I remember the jotter I used at school had to be used in every margin, covers, everywhere I could get a scribble I filled it. My uncle came to see us once or twice a week and gave us money for a new school book, but of course the money went on ice-cream!

'We only lasted four months and came back to Belfast in July. It was sad in the end to leave because I was seven by then and beginning to enjoy it, as I had made a lot of friends. But it was great to get home and see my father again and be with mother full time. I stayed in touch with some of the friends I made in Tyrone. I had started school with some of them when we first lived there, and having renewed our friendship in 1941, we stayed in touch.'

Today Gerry does not feel that his experiences as an evacuee affected him badly, despite all of the difficulties, and he feels that Mrs Martin did her best for him.

Gerry Mullan (right, as a baby) with his family. Gerry was sent to live with a friend of the family in 1941. (*Courtesy of Kevin Byers*)

Will We Starve?

Irene Wood, then aged 11, was evacuated from Salford to Hambleton, Lancashire, in September 1939.

Irene Wood (second from left) with her friends Edith, Betty and Ella, at Ryecroft Hall in 1939. (*Courtesy of Irene Wood Taylor*)

'We left Cross Lane Railway Station for Hambleton, near Poulton-Le-Fylde. We had our name tags, gas masks, and a small suitcase. We were given a paper carrier bag containing food items, among them a thick block of chocolate, a packet of biscuits and a packet of cream crackers. The mischievous older lads began shouting, "When this is gone, that's your lot. You're going to starve to death," which reduced some girls to tears.

'We arrived at the village hall to find sandwiches, grapes, apples and lemonade. It was the first time some of us poor Salford kids had eaten a grape, and the food was gone in less than ten minutes. My friends Edith,

Betty and Ella were housed with me at Ryecroft Hall, Hambleton, the home of the wealthy businessman, John W. Lewis. He was the son of John Tetlow Lewis, J.P. of Westfield House, Patricroft, sole proprietor of James Lewis and Company, with offices in Manchester, London, Glasgow and Belfast.

'Life there was very different from life in Salford! There was a gardener, cook-housekeeper, and Margaret, the maid, and the family owned a yacht, with a skipper who also served as the chauffeur. Mr Lewis commuted by train from Poulton-le-Fylde to Manchester, where he would stay for three days, then return to Hambleton for the remainder of the week. Tea was served a 4.30pm sharp, and dinner at 7pm.'

Irene recalls that her parents visited her every six weeks by bus, and that they paid seven shillings a week to the government for her keep at their local post office.

An English Education

In 1937, the Spanish Civil War caused Ester Laria, then aged seven, to be evacuated from the Basque region to England. The outbreak of war in 1939 meant that she could not return home to her parents.

Ester (second from the left) with her family in their garden, before the war. (*Courtesy of Ester Nickson*)

'In 1939 I went to live with Mr and Mrs Hope in Northampton. They were offered an allowance for having me, but said, "Send the money to suffering people in Spain." They were atheists but so Christian–like, they would help anybody.

'I attended Military Road School and the headmaster told everyone they had a little Spanish girl coming and had to be kind to her. On the first day, certain kids surrounded me and one boy with bright red hair kept poking me and saying, "Spanish onions, they're lovely". I said to him, "Don't do that little boy!" in a very posh voice. The third time he did it I said to him, "If you do it again little boy I will hit you," and he said, "Try it then," so I did and we had a fight on the floor! He tore the lapel off my coat, and I ended up with a handful of red hair.

'The next day a group of kids surrounded me again, but I was ready for them. I became good friends with a girl called Betty Andrews, who taught me to swear. She would say to me, "Say bloody", and I said it and she said "Oh you swore!" I thought she was teaching me English – well she was in a way! When I got home I was sitting at the dinner table, and asked Aunt and Uncle what the word meant. Aunt nearly choked, and she was at the school the very next day!'

Ester remained with the Hopes until she was 18 and today she still lives in England. At the age of 25, when she was married and expecting a baby, she visited her family in Spain. Her only regret is that she never really got to know her mother and father, but feels that they were just victims of circumstance.

From Ceylon to the Irish Coast

William Crawford, then aged 11, was evacuated from Belfast, Northern Ireland, to Portrush in 1942.

'I was born in Ceylon, where Dad worked in the colonial service. In 1937, during a holiday in Dublin, he left my sisters, Jean and Alison and I with relatives until his contract abroad ended. I attended Cabin Hill School, Belfast, and one day I turned on the wireless to hear news of the declaration of war. I was horrified because I knew my parents were a long way away, and might not be able to return until the end of Dad's contract.

'I experienced two air raids at school and on one occasion our Headmaster, 'Fluffy' Sutton, read Sherlock Holmes stories to us in the shelters. There was no latrine, so we were allowed out for a pee, although sometimes we used to pretend, and stay out just a bit too long to watch the bombs and the fires of Belfast. In 1942 our school moved to the safety of Portrush on the north coast, where we were accommodated in hotels and boarding houses.

'I had joined the school at the age of nine, barely able to read and write, but the masters and boys helped him me lot and this spurred me on to achieve. I also gained the respect of my peers because of my tales of living in the tropics of Ceylon, roaming the tea plantations and catching snakes.

'One morning in 1945, I was told to travel to my Uncle Hubert's house in Belfast to meet my parents. I entered the living room and saw two people, a man and a woman. The woman, my mother, asked, "Are you William?" I just nodded through teary eyes. Then Mother said to the man, "Matthew, are you going to say hello to William?" Matthew turned towards me and said "Are you my son?" My father and I shook hands, I didn't want to let go.'

William later attended Trinity College Dublin to study medicine and eventually became a Consultant Surgeon of Obstetrics and Gynaecology – not bad for a boy who could barely read and write at the age of nine.

William Crawford (right) cycling with his sisters Jean (left) and Alison (centre) in 1941. A year later William was evacuated to Portrush. (*Courtesy of Bruce Crawford*)

Lincoln's Legacy

Marjorie Escritt, then aged 13, was evacuated from Thoresby High School in Leeds to Lincoln.

'As we approached Lincoln by train, we saw the Cathedral built on the heights of Lincoln. The sun shone and it looked awesome. We were taken to Skellingthorpe and a girl from my form and I were billeted with a family in Brant Road. I did not like this girl, and horror of horrors, had to share a double bed with her. However, she became homesick and soon I became the single occupant with my host family, who were very kind to me.

'I learnt a lot during my evacuation, as I had to wash my own hair and make very personal decisions. Some pupils did not settle, or were not happy in their billets, so there was a constant dribble back to Leeds and our numbers depleted. We all went home for Christmas 1939 and, again, many girls did not return to Lincoln. There were 12 pupils in my form and we were housed in a newly-vacated set of old buildings on Lincoln Common. In February 1940, I took up residence with another kind couple in Usher Green. I also became great friends with a Lincoln girl.

'Lincoln was surrounded by RAF stations which attracted German bombers and slowly the war began to get nearer. When the Dunkirk evacuation took place, fears grew that we would be invaded by Germany. Our parents and the Leeds authorities decided that we should all go back home. We returned on 24 June 1940, to find that our old school was closed and we had to transfer to the other high school in Leeds.

Marjorie's friendship with the Lincoln girl endured after her return home, through letters and visits, until they both turned 80 years old.

Marjorie Escritt was evacuated to Lincoln and will never forget her first sight of Lincoln Cathedral. (*Courtesy of Marjorie Elliff, née Escritt*)

A Sense of Independence

James Henry Walter Humphries, then aged 14, was evacuated from Harringay, London, to Goonhavern in Cornwall.

'As London began to suffer the horrors of the Blitz, it was decided that my mother should leave London, as she was about to give birth. It was also decided that my brothers and I should be sent to safety in Cornwall. Harold was 12 and Ronnie was 6 and we endured a seven-hour train journey from Paddington Railway Station. Being the eldest, I felt it was my duty to look after my younger brothers during this traumatic time.

'Life as evacuees was very different for us boys. We had moved from a highly populated part of London to a quiet village in rural Cornwall. The school had smaller class sizes than we were used to, and Perranporth, with its sand dunes and seashore, was not far away. We kept ourselves occupied in our spare time, playing with the local children which was a great experience. I joined the local football team too, and the experiences of life in Cornwall stayed with us for the rest of our lives, providing us with a sense of independence. When we eventually returned to London we were presented with a new sister, Betty.'

Many years later, the family had many happy holidays in Goonhavern and the neighbouring village of Rose. They explored some of the places that James visited during the war, and also met some of the people he had known. Sadly James passed away in 1994 and his son Jim wishes that he had asked his father more about his time as an evacuee.

James Humphries (back row, second from the left) joined the local football team in Goonhavern. This photograph was taken in 1941. (*Courtesy of Jim Humphries*)

The Magic of Matlock

Doreen Holden, then aged seven, was evacuated with Mauldeth Road School, Burnage, Manchester, to Matlock, Derbyshire.

'I was taken into a manor house with Mum and two lads from my class. They put us in the nursery and we played with some children's toys. We were allowed in the kitchen and garden but not in some of the rooms. Mum stayed and made breakfast for us for a week, then she went home.

'One day, the man who owned the manor house shot himself because he was worried that he might go bankrupt due to the war. A nice couple on Starkholme Road took me in because my name was Doreen, the same as their little girl! They treated me very well, bought me dolls and made me jelly and custard because I hated rice pudding!

'The house was opposite Riber Castle and at night I sat in my bedroom, watching the castle in the moonlight. It was magical and felt like fairyland! I was always out playing with local children in the fresh air and made friends with a family nearby who had two children. We used to play in their attic at dressing up, as they had a trunk full of Edwardian clothes.

'One day the lady who looked after me was taken ill, so I was moved to the Paulsons who taught me to knit, sew and cook. My family visited every month or so, and at some point, the bombing eased off so Dad said "Let's bring her home." I didn't want to go home to a city estate, as I loved being in Matlock.'

When Doreen went home to Manchester she felt very claustrophobic, noticing the noisy buses and trains and smell of smoke in the air. She did not let her parents know how she felt.

Doreen Holden loved country life as an evacuee in Matlock and did not enjoy returning to the city streets of Manchester. (*Courtesy of Doreen Sheffield, née Holden*)

A Night to Remember

Lourdes Cavilla, then aged 10, was evacuated with her mother and five younger siblings, from Gibraltar to London, in July 1940.

This photograph was taken in Gibraltar, before Mrs Cavilla and her daughters were evacuated to England in July 1940. (*Courtesy of Lourdes Cavilla*)

'I think it was a 17-day journey to the United Kingdom, zigzagging due to U-boats. We were treated very kindly by the sailors, but it was very uncomfortable in the hold of the ship. I have hated boats ever since, especially the smell, though not so much the motion, which has stayed with me for life. We reached London and were delivered to a huge new hotel facing Hyde Park. We arrived tired, dirty and cold to a lovely welcome by our relations who were already there.

'I will never forget the hot bath, or the bed with the crisp white sheets and warm blankets. It was stable. No rocking! And no smell! It was a night to remember. We awoke on our first morning to the sound of music from buskers and people throwing money out of the window, what an experience!

'We soon got used to the new way of life, no cooking was allowed, everything was served hotel-style. Eventually the women revolted and bought little electric stoves and cooked Spanish food to their heart's content! The air raids were horrendous, but like everything else we soon got used to them – at first we would gather in the basement, which served for everything; meals, dances, concerts, playing, schooling and for praying when bombs were falling all around us. The building shook if there was a hit near by, the all–clear horn sounded and we would return to our rooms and get any possible rest.'

Although she found life in wartime London very frightening at times, Lourdes had a wonderful time during the war. She danced, sang at concerts and made lots of friends.

First View of the Sea

Rita Roberts, then aged six, was evacuated with St Thomas' School, Birmingham to Bromsgrove in September 1939.

'I remember feeling very sad and frightened; I thought I was many miles away from home. At that time Bromsgrove was all countryside, trees and fields with lovely big farm houses. I was one of the lucky ones chosen by a family who seemed quite wealthy. Mr King was a departmental head at the Austin Motor Company. Their house was called Blackmore Lodge, a large black and white country house with a plentiful garden. The Kings were very good to me, they bought me new clothes and nice books to read.

Rita Roberts gained a great love of the countryside because of her experiences in Bromsgrove. (*Courtesy of Rita Roberts*)

'Mr King often had to go away on business and we would all go with him, mostly to Wales. This was very exciting for me; with the exception of the car journey, as I suffered from car sickness. I was allowed to go to the farms where I saw what life on a farm was like. I got to help with milking cows, feeding chickens, collecting the eggs, making butter and cheese, having a ride on a horse, but the best thing was seeing a lamb born.

'Another exciting time was being taken to Aberystwyth in Wales to see the sea, which I had never done before. All I could say was "Ooh, look at all that water." To my surprise, Mr and Mrs King had bought me a brand new swimming costume, which I immediately changed into and ran splashing along the sea front.'

Rita recalls that during the holiday she had to learn to swim, so that the next time they visited Wales she wouldn't be afraid to make the most of the sea. Thanks to the Kings, at this point she gained a love of Wales and the countryside.

A Londoner in Blackpool

Jim Davey, then aged 11, attended Alleyn's School, in Dulwich, south London, which was evacuated to Rossall School, near Blackpool, in September 1943.

'During my first evacuation, I lived with the Bannister family in Horley, but in 1943 I was evacuated to Cleveleys. After breakfast we would walk along the sea front to Rossall School and in the evening we would return by tram. We were lucky to have full-time education and because we were, effectively, confined to the premises there were various entertainments going on in the evenings and at weekends. I remember seeing George Formby when he came to watch his nephew in the school boxing championships.

Jim Davey (left) and his sister Betty (second left) with Jim's first foster mother, Mrs Bannister and her son Donald. (*Courtesy of Jim Davey*)

'The first time that I went home for the holiday was Christmas 1943 and the train was four hours late. Our parents had been waiting at Euston Station all that time. It was a big wrench going back to school again.

'We were allowed to go into Cleveleys unaccompanied and visit the local cinema and even then some of the penny arcades and seaside attractions were open. Blackpool was only a tram ride away and was out of bounds, unless we could find a reason for going in. The usual excuse was 'It's my father/mother's birthday and I want to get something to send to him/her.' When we got there you would not believe that there was a war on. The Pleasure Beach was in full swing and there was even a shopkeeper boasting about the number of times he had been prosecuted for illegally selling ice cream, which was normally unobtainable.'

When Jim returned to Blackpool five years ago, he was surprised to see that it was not substantially any different from how he remembered it.

Life amongst the Coal Mines

Clifford Broughton, then aged six, was evacuated from Lewisham in south-east London to South Wales, in December 1940.

'My sister and brother were billeted with Blodwen Thomas, a miner's widow, at her house 'Glanpedol' in Twyn. In December the London Blitz intensified, so I went to join Mavis and John. Auntie Blod was very generous to accept all three of us and for that we were eternally grateful, because it lessened the blow of leaving our parents. It was a sea-change in culture, moving into a rural, Welsh-speaking mining community, but we were safe, save for the nights when Swansea was bombed in February 1941! We could hear the explosions even though we were 20 miles distant.

John Broughton (left) with his sister Mavis, their foster mother Mrs Blodwen Thomas and Clifford. (*Courtesy of the People of Cwmamman website*, www.cwmammanhistory.co.uk)

'Mum and Dad visited us alternately once a month. Considering that it was a seven-hour journey from Lewisham this was a tremendous effort on their behalf. The village was at the confluence of two rivers at the head of the Amman Valley. One of the rivers was known as the 'black river' because it was literally black from the colliery workings upstream. Auntie Blod's neighbours showed us how to kill chickens, and what with a pig slaughterhouse just down the road, we were certainly indoctrinated into country life. Although I only had a few Welsh friends – I think the evacuees tended to keep to their own – I learned a little Welsh before we returned home in April 1945.'

After the war, Auntie Blod and the Broughton family visited each other. Auntie Blod died in the 1980s and Cliff says that he will always be grateful for her love and affection during those wartime years.

Coming Home to the Doodlebugs

Mervyn Bailey, then aged five, was evacuated from London to Eccleston, Lancashire in 1943.

'I was firstly evacuated to Chichester then taken home again. I was there during the London Blitz but after some time I was sent to Eccleston. My new home was with Mr and Mrs Bateman who lived in the school house, in the grounds of the local school, as Mr Bateman was the headmaster.

'I made friends there, one of whom was Bobby Moon, the son of a farmer. This was a great adventure, in lots of ways for me, a boy coming from a town, never being close to animals, and the freedom to play about in haystacks was marvellous. I also played on the stepping stones which crossed a small stream in the village.

'I had a very happy time with the Batemans and the Moon family. My mother and Mrs Bateman wrote to each other and I still have one of their letters. After some time, my parents decided that it would be safe for me to return home, so I travelled back to Wimbledon. I was back home from the peace of the countryside, just in time for the V2 attacks. I actually saw one of the V1s or doodlebugs, fly low across our back garden before crashing into houses in Plough Lane. Another 100 yards and it would have exploded on the Wimbledon football pitch, causing no casualties. Such is fate!'

A few years ago Mervyn visited Eccleston and he was devastated to see that the school house had been demolished. However, the stepping stones were still there and it was a very emotional moment for him to stand on them again, 65 years later.

This photograph of Mervyn Bailey was taken during his first evacuation, to Chichester, in November 1939. (*Courtesy of Mervyn Bailey*)

A Life-long Fear of Water

Anthony Richards, then aged 10, was evacuated with his twin brother, from St Charles Roman Catholic School in Hull, to Stillington Hall, Yorkshire, in September 1939.

'I remember the beautiful house coming into view and we entered a large building at the rear of the Hall. There was a dormitory with 30 small camp beds in rows, a little cupboard next to each. In a corner, curtained off, was an area with a large double bed in which slept our guardian, a man called Jack Burke. I had never seen such a large bed just for one person, as I came from a family of eight, with dad dying, aged only 39, when we [Anthony and his twin brother] were just two years old. In two corners of the room were buckets for the usual...any noise was soon greeted by Jack's loud, masterly and intimidating voice!

'One thing that had a devastating effect on my life happened on an extremely hot day at Stillington Hall. Within the greenhouse, sunk into a corner, was a old tank filled with dirty water, eight feet deep. For some reason, probably because I was overheated, one of the Catholic priests, Brother Serenus, made me get into the tank. I clung desperately to the side, trying to keep my head above water as he kept dunking my head under, while saying in his French accent, "Go down again." I felt sick, frightened and could hardly get my breath. Eventually it stopped but left me petrified as I couldn't swim – I'd never even been to the baths in 1939!'

When the boys passed their Eleven Plus examination, they left Stillington Hall. Later, Anthony married his childhood sweetheart and they had three children. He is still terrified of water!

Stillington Hall, where Anthony Richard had an unforgettable experience with an old water tank. (*Courtesy of Stillington and District Community Archive* www. stillingtoncommunityarchive.org)

A Fairytale Palace

Jessica Young, then aged eight and originally from London, was evacuated from Selsey Camp in West Sussex, with 200 disabled girls, to Peckforton Castle, Cheshire, in August 1940.

'We left Selsey at 8am and at 10pm we drove up a dark, tree clad drive to a full sized 80-roomed castle, all dark and shadowy. As we entered the castle in the dark because of the blackout, Mrs Thomas reassured us by saying, "Now the dark is like blind man's buff, so hold on to the one in front."

'With a teacher holding a torch to show the way, we went down the spiral steps, leading down into the long corridor which went the

Peckforton Castle in Cheshire. When Jessica Young was evacuated to Peckforton, she described it as 'a fairy tale palace'. (*Author's collection*)

whole length of the castle. We passed lots of rooms until we reached the big servants dining hall, which had one long table nearly the length of it and lots of trestle tables with forms for eight children to sit at. The walls were white washed and decorated with heads of foxes, deer and antlers.

'A local potter had made us all a pretty flower mug each, in several designs, they now contained soup. How good it tasted with a thick slice of bread to eat with it. After supper we climbed another staircase and got into bed. We slept that night in vest and pants, not knowing where we were, too tired to care, and hundreds of miles away from our families. In the morning I looked out of the window, it was lovely, like a fairy tale palace, all glistening pink stone. We spent our first two weeks learning how to climb the stairs as some girls wore callipers.'

Jessica spent five years at Peckforton Castle and later she wrote her life story, including details of her evacuation. She dedicated it to Mrs Thomas, who gave the children such loving care.

A wartime Oxo advertisement featuring evacuees. (*Author's collection*)

Bob Cooper, then aged seven, was evacuated from Islington to Ladynance in Cornwall in 1940.

'I was sitting in a big hall next to Billy Shipman, who I had just made friends with. We were both chosen by Mr and Mrs Old who lived in a tiny hamlet called Ladynance, near Colan in Cornwall. Mr Old was a farm labourer and he worked really hard, he had to plough the fields using a horse, milk the cows and look after the farm. He was strong as an ox but I never enjoyed the hard work that farming entailed – Billy and I used to pick potatoes and help out on the farm. Mrs Old did the cooking and made Cornish pasties, and food was a bit tight. They looked after us well and I called them 'Auntie' and 'Uncle'.

'On our first day there, Billy and I went out for a wander and as we were passing some trees we heard a noise overhead and looked up – it was the local children looking down on us as if we were from outer space! We had never seen green fields before and at night the sky was so clear that you could see hundreds of stars. Mr and Mrs Old had no gas, electricity or running water, we collected water from a well, and used a bucket for a toilet. It was normal to them but very strange to me!

'I returned home some time in 1943 – one day Dad was walking towards me with a big smile on his face, and he took me back to London.'

Bob's old house had been damaged by bombs, so the family moved into a house in Dalston, east London. Because he had picked up a Cornish accent during his evacuation, Bob felt he stood out a bit, but he says that he was able to stand up for himself and soon lost the accent again.

This photograph of Bob Cooper and his puppy was taken in Islington before he was evacuated to Cornwall. (*Courtesy of Bob Cooper*)

The German in the Woods

James Roffey, then aged 10, and his brother John, aged 11, were evacuated from Camberwell, south London, to Pulborough, West Sussex, in September 1939.

James Roffey (right) and his brother John (left) during the war. (*Courtesy of James Roffey*)

'John and I were always exploring the countryside, and we built a den in the woods where we always kept a supply of apples. One day we found that our apples had been stolen and assumed that the village boys had taken them. Then my brother said "There is a man hiding behind the trees." He looked to be a young man, one leg of his trousers was torn and bloodstained, parts of what looked like a parachute were tangled in the bushes. We assumed he was a German and ran to the village to tell someone about him.

'I was billeted in the general shop and ran in, shouting, "There is a German hiding in the woods!" to which my foster father sighed and said, "Oh you boys and your stories! Go away and play!" Eventually a man said

"I'm going past the police house. Perhaps I'll call in, just in case the boys are right." Later the policemen and Home Guard returned with the German airman, who was so badly wounded they had laid him on the floor of their van. We later heard he had indeed bailed out from his badly damaged plane, two days earlier, with only our apples to eat. Did anyone thank we boys? No, of course not.'

During evacuation James suffered from homesickness and he always wanted to go home. However, when that finally happened, after four years, he found to his surprise that he was unable to re-adjust to life in London. A few years after leaving school, he returned to Pulborough to live and work there. After taking early retirement, he formed, and still manages, the Evacuees Reunion Association.

Someone here is going to need your help

Johnny lives in the city. His home may seem safe enough now. But if raids come it will be another matter. Johnny must be moved. It is unthinkable that he should be left to take his chance among the horrors of modern bombing warfare.

The Government is going to send Johnny to your district if raids come. This is where your help is needed. To promise now to give Johnny a home, so that the authorities may know he will be cared for. Do not think that because we have not been raided yet, we are not likely to be.

As the year grows older the danger does not grow less. These children in the city may be needing a safe home next month, next week, perhaps tomorrow. When they do, they will need it suddenly, urgently, desperately.

All you need do is enrol your name with your local Authority. You may be asked to take a child now, or your name may be kept against the time when raids make a second evacuation necessary. When you enrol, you will be doing a splendid service for the nation.

The Minister of Health, who has been entrusted by the Government with the conduct of evacuation, asks you urgently to join the Roll of those who are willing to receive children. Please apply to your Local Council.

Government evacuation advertisement in wartime newspaper. (*Author's collection*)

Chapter Three

The Kindness of Strangers:
Wartime Foster Parents and Carers

The stories within this chapter illustrate the kindness shown to many evacuees by the foster parents who took them in, as well as the local people who befriended them and offered their help. There is no official figure for the number of people who had evacuees billeted in their homes and, at the time, some were certainly more willing to do so than others.

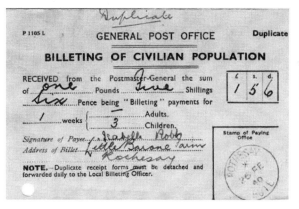

Evacuee billeting receipt. (*Courtesy of Argyll and Bute Council Archives*)

In 1938, the Government had instructed every council to undertake a survey to ascertain how many evacuees could be accommodated in the local area. A document issued by Retford Rural District Council in September 1938 stated that these households were to include 'inhabited houses of all classes, whether mansions, villas, bungalows or cottages, and will include householders of every station in life, without exception'. Each householder was advised that it was compulsory to take in evacuees and that billeting allowances would be provided.

During interviews with evacuees, it was clear that some evacuees were not wanted by the people they were billeted with, and wartime newspapers include reports of households who refused to take them in. Luckily, countless others flocked to help these displaced adults and children. One elderly Lancashire man, John Fletcher, even became 'Father Christmas' to hundreds of evacuees in the town of Bury, Lancashire.

Today, many evacuees still fondly remember the loving, life-long friendships that they formed with their foster families.

I Didn't Want to Go Home!

Adelaide Harris, then aged five, was evacuated from Hull to Billingborough, Lincolnshire, in September 1939.

Adelaide Harris grew to love the Wright family, who cared for her in Billingborough during the war. (*Courtesy of Adelaide Palmer, née Harris*)

'We were evacuated with our school and travelled a long way from Hull to Billingborough. We went into the school hall where people came to look at us, then picked us. Me and two other girls were chosen by a butcher, then I was moved to the home of Mr and Mrs Wright and their daughter Renee. They were a lovely family and I called Mrs Wright 'Mum'. I got on really well with Renee, who was older then me. She looked after me, and I felt like I was their own daughter. Mrs Wright also had lovely dresses made for me.

'The local people were very friendly to us evacuees, as was everyone at the school. I really loved the country air, and we were never short of fruit and veg. I used to collect water from a tap on the side of the lane, and they had a toilet in the garden but it didn't flush. An American Air Force base nearby organised Christmas parties for us.

'During this time, my Dad joined the navy on a minesweeper, and Mum came to visit me several times. Mr Wright worked on the railways and unfortunately he was killed whilst at work. Mrs Wright was pregnant with her son Arthur, and she still kept me, despite losing her husband. I really took to Arthur when he was born. When our school was sent home at the end of the war I didn't want to go. I was so used to living with Mrs Wright.'

When Adelaide returned home, she cried for days and she missed Arthur and Renee very badly. In the photograph above, Adelaide is wearing one of the dresses Mrs Wright had made for her.

A Runaway Evacuee

Dennis Camp, then aged four, was evacuated from Guernsey with his mother, Agnes, to Yorkshire, then to Stockport.

'In Stockport I caught pneumonia and was sent to a Blackpool hospital where injured soldiers from Dunkirk were coming in. The hospital contacted Mum to say that I was on the verge of death. She visited as soon as she could, then sadly told me, "I can't stay here with you, as I have no money to pay for a boarding house."

'The soldiers in my ward heard about Mum's situation and handed me all their pennies and two pence pieces, which I gave to Mum so she could stay in Blackpool. The soldiers constantly prayed for me and I firmly believe that it was with their help that I survived.

Dennis Camp, pictured after the war, aged 10. (*Courtesy of Karen Frith*)

'I was ill on and off throughout the war and at one point was sent to a hospital in Teignmouth, Devon. I made friends with another boy, Richard Goman, and after a while, we became unhappy with the treatment there, and decided to run away. Richard made his way to Wales and I managed to make my way back to Stockport. Mum had moved into a cottage by then and I somehow managed to find her. It only had half a roof and the landlord, Mr Murdoch, had knocked on the door saying "This place is condemned, Mrs Camp!" Mum had replied, "Well, I have nowhere else to go," and he replied "Well, for your pluck, I will have the roof done!"'

Sadly, Dennis passed away in August 2013, soon after this interview. The cottage in Stockport is still standing today, even though it was condemned in the 1940s.

An Evacuee From Nazi Germany: Part One

Wolfgang Plessner, then aged 14, was evacuated from Nazi Germany to Bury, Lancashire, in February 1939.

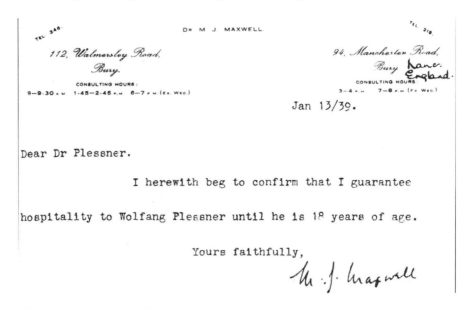

This letter was written by Dr Maxwell to Dr Plessner in Germany, confirming that he would care for Dr Plessner's son, Wolfgang, in England. (*Courtesy of Manchester Archives*)

'Due to persecution of Jewish families in Germany at the time, my parents were invited to send me to study at Bury Grammar School in England. Mother put me on a train in Berlin and I was later put onto a Manchester train at Euston. Dr Maxwell, my foster father, picked me up and we drove to our home in Bury.

'I was extremely fortunate in having been placed with a warm-hearted Jewish doctor's family, similar to my own. Their son Victor was aged nine and he also went to the grammar school, but Elaine was only five. Within a few weeks I had learnt more English from Victor, Elaine and their parents than I had learnt at school in Germany in the previous two years.

'After the first few months I had very little trouble understanding what the masters were saying, but most of the boys were speaking with such thick

Lancashire accents that it took me a long time, perhaps over a year, to follow what they were trying to tell me. With the help of a little string-pulling by my headmaster, my parents were fortunate to obtain a visa for England just before war broke out in September 1939. They came with little financial means and I stayed with my foster parents for another year, then joined my parents in their small flat in Bury.'

Wolfgang later passed his A-levels and won a scholarship to study Engineering at Manchester University.

Wolfgang Plessner pictured in Germany, 1933. (*Courtesy of Susan Plessner*)

An Evacuee From Nazi Germany: Part Two

Victor Maxwell was nine years old when Wolfgang Plessner, a Jewish refugee from Germany, came to live with his family in Bury, Lancashire.

Victor Maxwell (left) making sandcastles on the beach with Wolfgang Plessner (right). (*Courtesy of Victor Maxwell*)

'In 1936 one of the governors of Bury Grammar School had been involved in arrangements to bring over a number of Jewish academics to posts at Manchester University. In Breslau she had come into contact with Dr and Mrs Plessner and when, in 1937, the school decided to sponsor four Jewish boys and four girls, she approached the Plessners. They arranged that Wolfgang, then 14, should come and live with us and he arrived in February 1939 when I was 9.

'The promise to give a home for three years to a strange boy was not an empty one. I remember meeting this lone figure off the train at London Road Station and how he was transfixed by the orange fluorescent street lights as we drove home to Bury. Wolfgang was tall, slim, and shy. A few days after he arrived he came down to breakfast with gifts for all of us. "It is my birthday," he said "and at home it is usual to give presents not receive them." He gave me a pearl-handled penknife, which I still use.

'He settled into school with some difficulty but was very bright and adapted to his new environment. He was deft with his hands and we created a workshop for him, where he taught me some of his skills. He was studious and left school with a prestigious scholarship, which took him to Manchester University to study electrical engineering and he left with honours. He went on to marry a doctor's daughter, also a refugee, and had a very successful career working on semi-conductors.'

Wolfgang retired to Aldeburgh in Suffolk, and became a familiar figure locally, cycling around at high speed with his coat tails flying. He died in an accident, aged 83, when knocked off his bicycle by a carelessly opened car door.

War Can't Stop Father Christmas

Mr John Fletcher, then aged 72, became 'Father Christmas' to hundreds of Channel Island evacuees in Bury, Lancashire. John's grandson, Ron Standring, has shared this story.

John Fletcher (centre, rear) in post-war Guernsey, reunited with some of the evacuees he had befriended in Bury. (*Courtesy of Margaret Cornick*)

'When the Channel Island children arrived, my grandfather felt a great sympathy for these kiddies. He realised that they would not receive any Christmas presents from their families, who were still in the occupied Channel Islands. He wondered what he could do to help brighten and cheer these children's lives on their first Christmas in a strange land. He decided to raise funds so that gifts could be bought for them. He wrote letters stating what he wanted to do and sent them to hundreds of friends in the United

States and Canada, whom he had visited since he retired from working as a commercial traveller. And also to others in Australia and New Zealand. They all sent donations willingly!

'In December 1940 he arranged a Christmas party at which, dressed as Father Christmas, he presented 200 children with gift parcels. Throughout the war, he continued this work, purchasing at least 300 parcels every year. In May 1945 he shared the evacuees' joy when the Channel Islands were liberated from German occupation and organised a 'farewell party' for them just before they returned home.'

John Fletcher visited Guernsey after the war, and was reunited with many of the evacuees. He died in February 1953, but is fondly remembered by the children who knew him. One former evacuee, Barbara Mechem, recalls, 'the only Christmas presents I received during the whole of the war were given to me by Mr Fletcher'. The full story of John Fletcher can be found in Gillian Mawson's previous book, *Guernsey Evacuees*, (2012).

Family Friendship

Eileen Farrell, then aged seven, was evacuated from New Moston, Manchester, to Hepstonstall in Yorkshire.

Eileen Farrell (right) had to leave her sister Sheila (left) behind when she was evacuated to Yorkshire. (*Courtesy of Sheila Worrall*)

'I attended New Moston Primary School and, at some point, was evacuated to live with a lovely family in Heptonstall. Dick and Cis Greenwood lived at 2 Silver Street, and they had a daughter, Pat, of a very similar age to me.

'I attended the local school with Pat and also went to the Sunday School at Heptonstall Church. The family made me so very welcome and I was very happy there. Dick Greenwood worked in a local factory and eventually died from either asbestosis or something similar that was caused by his work. Pat became a seamstress in one of the local factories.

'My mum and dad were still in Manchester during this time and when things got really bad there due to air raids, they would take my little sister Sheila to stay with friends in St Annes, Lancashire, until things had settled down again. After the war, the friendship between our families continued. Pat and I went on holiday together and we made regular visits to the Greenwoods during the year.'

Sadly, Eileen developed a very rare medical condition and died when she was just 36. However, her sister Sheila always kept in touch with Pat on her behalf, until Pat's death in 1994.

A Tale of Two Sisters

Jean Flannery's Aunt Nellie and Uncle Reg Cutts lived in Bletchley, Buckinghamshire, and looked after evacuees Joan and Marjorie Hart, then aged eight and four, from Chiswick, London.

Nellie Cutts (left, holding Jean) with evacuees Marj and Joan Hart and husband Reg, in March 1945. (*Courtesy of Jean Flannery*)

'There was a houseful in my Aunt and Uncle's three-bedroom Cambridge Street home! Along with my mother Kitty, my father (when rarely home on leave), and me, they looked after Joan and Marjorie (Marj). Both were loved and were apparently thrilled when I was born! When my mother went into labour they were sent to stay with a neighbour, coming back to the surprise of a new baby.

'Marj was her mother's favourite and she really missed home. However, Joan, the elder, loved living in Bletchley. She was very happy there and told me later that she could do nothing right for her mother. Even as a young girl she had to scrub a long tiled hallway on a Saturday morning, along with other chores. Marj was allowed out to play, but Joan was kept in until she had cleaned the floor to her mother's satisfaction. With us, she was allowed to just be a child.

'The girls' parents would visit by train and the front room was turned into their bedroom. They brought us treats and my uncle, being a butcher, made sure they didn't leave empty handed! After the war Joan did not want to go back to London. She felt quite out of place at home and miserable at school. She said that her days in Bletchley were the happiest of her childhood.'

The families kept in touch after the war. Joan always considered herself a member of Jean's family, attending both family celebrations and funerals. Sadly, Joan now has dementia and is cared for by her husband. Marjorie died in 2012.

An Air-Raid Far From Home

Jean Pare, then aged 13, was evacuated with Yardley Grammar School, Birmingham, to Lydney, Gloucestershire, in September 1939.

Evacuees and teachers leaving Birmingham Moor Street Station in 1939. (*Courtesy of the Birmingham Mail*)

'I was very lucky as my new home was with a couple who had no children of their own, living in a pretty cottage. They were called Mr and Mrs H., but I was soon told to call them Auntie Lil and Uncle Bill. Once a month a Midland Red coach from Digbeth Coach Station came to Lydney for the day, bringing families to see their sons and daughters. My mother came every time and she got on well with Auntie Lil and Uncle Bill.

'One night in May 1940, I heard the engine of an aeroplane followed by an air-raid warning. I was really frightened by that noise and tiptoed downstairs to hide behind the settee! We heard later that the engine noise was a German bomber which had previously bombed Bristol. It was later shot down in the Bristol Channel. By June 1940 I had become very homesick and at the end of term in July I returned home to Birmingham.'

Jean's friendship with Uncle Bill and Auntie Lil continued after the war and she spent numerous holidays and weekends with them. When they died, Jean attended their funerals in Lydney. In 1989 Jean returned to Lydney, on a trip organised by the *Birmingham Post and Mail*, with two other evacuees. Jean also placed flowers on her foster parents' graves.

The Tricycle Thief

John Girard Andre, then aged 21 months, was evacuated from Guernsey to Burnley, Lancashire, with his mother in June 1940.

'We were billeted with May and Jim Clark in Hershel Street. Mum worked as a cleaner for the vicar and his wife and we spent most days at the vicarage. There was a good-humoured feud ongoing between them, as Mum was a staunch Methodist and would tease the vicar about him wearing a dress on Sundays etc.

'On one occasion he took me out in his big Rover car to a garage and they put the car up on the servicing lift. I remained in the car but was taken short whilst up in the air. I was too frightened to point out my predicament. I got a stern talking to but I was allowed in the car later on. I think I must have been about three then.

'I made friends with Michael, the son of the Woolworths manager, but one day Michael stole my tricycle. I told mum, she told Michael's mum, and Michael was to bring it back to our house the next day. Hershel Street was on a steep slope so the houses had many steps up to the front doors, but the front garden was at the house level so the steps were in an enclosed passage. I prepared to receive Michael by fetching the long wooden clothes prop and waiting for him to appear with the tricycle. On his arrival I swung the clothes prop with vigour and swept him clean off the tricycle into the middle of the road. He ran home screaming and I retrieved my tricycle. We still were friends, after a short recovery period.'

John and his Mum returned to Guernsey in 1945 and for many years they kept in contact with their friends in Burnley.

John Andre and his mother were evacuated from Guernsey and happily billeted with Mr and Mrs Clark in Burnley. (*Courtesy of John Andre*)

Two Adopted Aunts

Douglas Wood, then aged four, was evacuated from Birmingham to Rolleston-on-Dove, Staffordshire, in February 1940.

Douglas Wood (seated with Edith Ashmall) found a loving home with the Ashmall sisters. Edith's brother and her sister Kate are also pictured. (*Courtesy of Douglas Wood*)

'I was evacuated with my brother, but in Rolleston we were placed with separate families. I was chosen by Miss Ashmall (Auntie Edith) a middle-aged spinster who lived with her elderly maiden aunt (Auntie Kate). They had a large Victorian house, comfortable and warm, with a very large garden and I stayed with them for four very happy years.

'During my evacuation I saw my mother twice and my father once. On the day they visited me together they walked past me in the street, as they did not recognise me. On 23 November 1944, a taxi arrived in Rolleston to take me home to Birmingham. It was a very tearful farewell indeed – I did not want to leave my aunts, and they did not want me to go.

'Going home was a very traumatic and sad experience. I did not have a Birmingham accent and this was the subject of much ridicule. I had lost all affinity with my family, so there was no love or affection and when my father returned from war service the situation became worse, with some violent domestic disputes. He eventually left when I was 13 years old.

'I remained constantly in touch with my two aunts. Auntie Kate died in 1949, but I continued to visit Auntie Edith. She came to my wedding and my twenty-fifth wedding anniversary. I visited her just a few days before she died in 1989, three months before her hundredth birthday.'

For Douglas, being an evacuee with his lovely 'aunts' changed the course of his life. They will never be forgotten.

A Paper Trail for Parents

Peter Staples, then aged eight, was evacuated from the East End of London to Brumstead, near Stalham, North Norfolk.

'I was allocated with another boy, Donald Self, to a wealthy couple who owned a huge house and two cars – a Jaguar and a Vauxhall – which was unheard of at the time. Later they had to move to Thetford and wanted to take us with them. My Mum was not keen, as we would be separated from the rest of our school friends. Instead Donald and I went to live with Mr and Mrs Scarff in Brumstead, near Stalham. He was a cowman at a local farm and the couple had two sons, Patrick aged 10, and Derek aged 14.

'They had no gas or electricity, drew water from a well and cooked on a primus stove and range, which shocked my Mum when she came to visit. Despite this basic existence, they were a delightful family and it was great fun for us boys! Local signposts had been removed, so when my parents visited I wrote 'Old Rectory Lane' on pieces of paper and placed them in hedges, so my parents could follow them and find us. When they returned home I cried, but was soon fine as there was so much to keep me occupied.

'My evacuation experiences made me adaptable, which served me well in later life. After a year the authorities wanted to move us to Wales but Mum decided I should go home to London – just as the Blitz began! In 1941 a German aircraft dropped a bomb on a nearby railway bridge. Dad was driving over it and his car was peppered with shrapnel. His hip was badly shattered.'

Peter stayed in touch with the Scarffs and, on one occasion he visited with three friends, presenting Mrs Scarff with a box of chocolates.

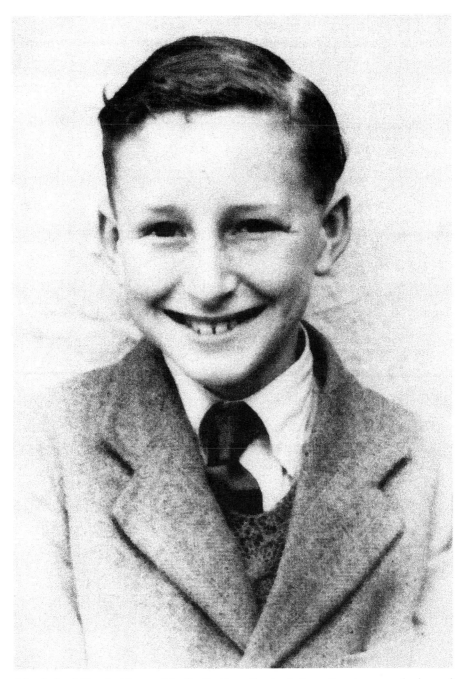

After being billeted with a wealthy family, Peter Staples had to adjust to a more basic rural life in North Norfolk. (*Courtesy of Peter Staples*)

Christmas Far From Home

Pamela Le Poidevin, then aged six, was evacuated from Guernsey to Stockport in June 1940.

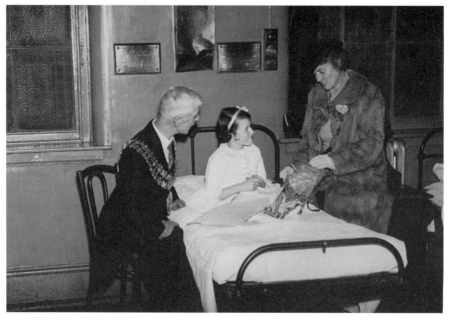

Pamela Le Poidevin spent Christmas in a Stockport hospital where she met the Mayor and his wife. (*Courtesy of Pamela Le Poidevin*)

'On Christmas Day 1942 I was ill in Stockport Infirmary. I told the nurses I was an evacuee from Guernsey, and they realised that I was not going to receive any Christmas presents from home. There was a scramble to find some things for me from Father Christmas! We also received a visit from the Mayor and Lady Mayoress of Stockport.'

Pamela managed to send a Red Cross message to her family in January 1943 to tell them that she had been in hospital.

Part of the Family

Judy Jones's family lived in Wales and looked after evacuees Roger and Ruth Davy, from Gosport.

'I was born in 1942 and during the war Mum and I lived at my auntie's house, situated between Mold and Denbigh, because my dad was in the navy. Roger and Ruth lived in the house with my uncle and aunt, Mum, me and four cousins, so there was quite a crowd of us! We had no gas or electricity and only cold water – any hot water was boiled on the fire. We did not have a bath and the lavatory was in the back yard.

Ruth Davy and her brother Roger found a loving home with Mrs Jones (right). Their father is pictured with them. (*Courtesy of Judy Fox*)

'Roger and Ruth went to school with my cousins, and were treated exactly the same way as we were, as a part of the family. They were taken everywhere with us, and included on days out to Rhyl. Their mum and dad used to visit them now and again and they too became part of our extended family – "Uncle Don" and "Auntie Betty".'

After the war, Judy's family remained in touch with Roger and Ruth, visiting them in Gosport. Ruth was later godmother to Judy's sister and Roger visited the Jones family when he was on holiday from university. Ruth and her fiancé Harry used to come and stay with the Jones family and Judy's family attended their wedding in Gosport.

Flight from France

Pierre Ratcliffe, then aged five, was evacuated with his family on HMS *Venomous*, sailing from Calais to London in May 1940.

'The Germans were not far from our village, so we collected a few belongings and joined other people going south. At Calais, there was a ship evacuating British citizens – Dad was British, so we had passports and could go on board. The authorities in England were marvellous and the WVS (Women's Voluntary Service) was, of course, there. These splendid middle class English ladies were dishing out tea and food. They all smelled of lavender!

Pierre Ratcliffe (front left) with his parents and sister Giselle, fled to England from Calais in May 1940. (*Courtesy of the HMS* Venomous *website*, www.holywellhousepublishing.co.uk/Ratcliffe.html)

'We were sent to a large terraced building in London where there were refugees like us. Dad had a chat with a civil servant and told him he had a sister in Leeds, so we went there by train. Auntie Pattie, Uncle Jack and Gram'ma were very surprised when they opened their door. They seemed to have no idea that conditions were so bad in France. I went into the street and, being a chatterbox, I was soon talking away in French to a group of children. I came back in the house and announced that all the children were deaf!

'Dad got a job in Newark-on-Trent. He told a bus conductor that he had found a job but had nowhere for his family to live. The man generously said we could stay with him and his wife. Later we returned to Leeds and rented a flat above a shop in Meanwood. I went to school and we were not far from Auntie Pattie, Uncle Jack and Gram'ma.'

When the family returned to Calais in January 1946, Pierre, the little chatterbox who had known no English, had forgotten his French, but he was a bright boy and soon caught up.

Talking Like a 'Carrot Cruncher'

Len Page, then aged eight, was evacuated with his twin sisters from London to Chipping Norton in 1940.

Evacuees arriving in Chipping Norton in 1940. (*Courtesy of Andy Parsons*, www.wargunner. co.uk/evacuee.htm)

'My sisters went to number 6 Chapel House, whilst I went to number 7, to Mr and Mrs Knight (Harry and Ada) and their son, Dennis. Harry was a wartime special policeman, but before the war ended he joined the fire brigade near London. Ada was a constant puffer of fags and loved whist drives, she always boasted that she had never had to buy a chicken for Christmas dinner, as she always won one at the whist drive.

'Evacuees were not as plentiful in Chippy, so the Londoners were easily integrated with the other school children and soon I was talking like the 'Carrot Crunchers', with plenty of sun and fresh air, helping at hay-making time in the fields of Hartley's farm during the school holidays. One day a bomb was dropped near a pig farm and I think that every child in Chippy made the pilgrimage to see the crater the bomb had left.

'The toilet was outside, no flush cistern but a bucket, which Mr. Knight emptied once a week and buried in a trench in the allotment. You never saw him empty the bucket and only knew it had been emptied by the large cabbage leaves that lined the bottom of the bucket. When I returned to London it took quite a time (and reminders) to learn to pull the chain again.'

After the war, Len kept in touch with the Knights. He visited in 1987, three weeks before Harry passed away. Len thought of Harry as his second dad and Harry always introduced Len to his friends as 'My little evacuee from London.'

Standing on Our Own Two Feet

Doreen Frisby, then aged 12, was evacuated with Walworth Central School to Sturminster Newton, Dorset, in September 1939.

'A boy scout took me and another pupil, Joyce, to the home of Mr Steve and Mrs Vi Goddard. It was a two-up, two-down thatched cottage. We often wonder what Vi thought of the two London girls standing on her doorstep, one 11 years old and one 12. They were brave to take us, as they were only in their twenties and had been married just a short while. There was no definite place that we could call 'school', so we spent a lot of time walking between the village hall, known as 'The Hut', and other buildings for our different lessons.

'In June 1940 our school occupied some of the manor house buildings which belonged to the local Squire, at Hinton St Mary, a mile and a half away. In spite of needing clothing coupons, we managed to keep in uniform, although there were some small changes. Our teachers (wonderful ladies) tried to maintain the standard as in pre-war London, both in appearance and with lessons.

'Joyce and I became firm friends. She returned home in 1942, whilst I finished my education and returned home in 1943.'

Doreen appreciates that she and her school friends had to stand on their own two feet, which created a permanent bond. The pupils placed a garden seat outside the village hall, dedicated to the villagers who took them in, and planted a tree in the garden of remembrance for their teachers.

Doreen Frisby was taken in by newly-weds Stephen and Violet Goddard, in Dorset. (*Courtesy of Daryl Chandler and Sue Heys*)

A Firm Friendship

Pam Buckley, then aged nine, was evacuated with her family from Jersey to Bury, Lancashire, in June 1940.

'When we arrived, Mum and Dad had a pillowcase with a few possessions inside, my sister had a book, my baby brother had a rattle and I had a doll. We were lucky because we were given a brand new house on an estate called Chesham Fold. We lived at 89 Goldfinch Drive and my cousins moved into 84. There were other Channel Islanders on the estate, plus a group of London evacuees who were lovely people but their house was absolutely filthy.

'Over the next five years I formed a great friendship with Audrey Davies, who lived across the road. In 1945 Jersey was liberated from the Germans and my family decided to return home, so Audrey and I tearfully said goodbye to each other and promised to stay in touch. She gave me a little brooch to remember her by, which I still have.

'For 36 years we exchanged photographs and gifts, but we lost touch when Audrey moved from Chesham to Radcliffe and I moved from Jersey to New Zealand. I continued to write to her old address, not knowing that she had moved, and of course received no reply.'

Many years later, Pam and Audrey were reunited. Audrey's great-grandson was being christened in Bury and a relative of her son-in-law flew from Jersey to attend. He turned out to be Pam's cousin and he was able to put the two friends back in touch with each other.

Channel Island evacuees outside Danesmoor House near Bury, Lancashire. (*Courtesy of Bury Archives*)

Auntie Bee and Uncle Bob

Mary Draper, then aged five, and her sister Vi, then aged three, were evacuated from Lowestoft to Chesterfield, Derbyshire, in June 1940.

'Vi and I were evacuated with our school and were taken to Barlborough, near Chesterfield. We had no Mum, and our Dad was in the Home Guard. A lovely couple took us into their home. Mr and Mrs Bacon had no children of their own, and they practically became our Mum and Dad until the day they died. The war really did us a favour because they were marvellous to us, treating us like little princesses.

'We called them Auntie Bee and Uncle Bob. They had a lovely home and we lived with them until the end of the war. When we had to leave them to return to Lowestoft, it broke our hearts as well as theirs. Our real Dad passed away when we were in our teens. I was with my fiancé by then, so my sister moved back to live with Mr and Mrs Bacon.'

Vi Draper (left) and her sister Mary (right) found a new family when they were evacuated to Derbyshire. (*Courtesy of Mary Draper*)

When Mary got married, her children looked upon Mr and Mrs Bacon as their grandparents. Vi still lives in Chesterfield, as does Mary's son Michael and Mary's family visit regularly.

An Idyllic Country Childhood

Harry Flack, then aged six, was evacuated from Blackheath, South London, to Petrockstowe, Devon, in May 1940.

'I was cared for by Fred and Winnie Cooper, who were in their forties. They were the most welcoming people who took me me into their home and hearts. There was no running water, gas and electricity, and the radio ran on an 'accumulator', which was changed each month by a delivery man. My particular job was to collect two ewers of water from a hand pump, on the roadside, some hundred yards or so from the cottage. I thought that it was great to be useful to this (in my eyes) elderly couple.

Petrockstowe Railway Station where Harry Flack spent many happy hours on the footplate of steam engines. (*Courtesy of the Petrockstowe website*, http://petrockstowevillage.co.uk)

'Fred was the local Station Master, so I had a great time on the footplate of the steam engines. I often 'drove' them – there was no 'Health and Safety' in 1940. I went round with Mrs Cooper's brother, Frank Marshall, to inspect rabbit traps and rode around the farm on his horse and cart. I collected the milk from the farm, helped with the harvest, and enjoyed having the loveliest of fresh food cooked on a kitchen range. It was wonderful!

'When I returned home at the end of 1941, I had very mixed feelings. Air raids in London had calmed down and my mother, naturally, wanted me back.'

In 1944, when the V1 rockets were launched on London, Mr and Mrs Cooper took Harry in again for six months. He last saw them in the 1960s before losing contact. However, Harry still remembers them with great affection.

Portsmouth evacuees board buses to the Isle of Wight ferry during an evacuation rehersal. (*Courtesy of The News, Portsmouth and The Home Front Museum, Llandudno*)

Chapter Four

Suffer the Little Children:
Homesickness and Heartbreak – the Darker
Side of Evacuation

Some of these stories make very difficult reading. Although many evacuees received loving care from their wartime foster parents, others did not. In 1939, only four female Ministry of Health inspectors had attended conferences on evacuation, contributing to the failure to foresee the conditions in which mothers and children would arrive, and the kind of services they would require. There were not enough local officials available to regularly inspect evacuees' billets, so problems were not always picked up.

Guernsey evacuee mother and children at Weymouth. (*Courtesy of Guernsey Press*)

Many evacuees recall that, if a billeting officer did visit their foster home, then the child was rarely asked if they were happy, or even spoken to. In some cases, evacuees who were ill-treated were only rescued because a neighbour had observed the situation and contacted the authorities. In other cases, their teachers contacted the authorities after observing bruises and marks, or after gently questioning a child about their obvious unhappiness.

The authorities organising evacuation failed to appreciate the psychological repercussions of being moved into the homes of strangers for children and also adults. This chapter focuses on the more troubling aspects of evacuation, and reveals the negative effects that resulted from children being sent far from home to sometimes unsuitable foster parents. Here are stories of physical and mental abuse and even children who were treated as servants. Despite being sent to safety from wartime bombing, some evacuees still witnessed other forms of death and destruction. Many lost loved ones in air raids or as a result of infectious diseases.

Despite the traumatic nature of these stories, the evacuees want them to be told today to represent the full picture of evacuation in World War Two.

Wartime Separation and Bereavement

Brian Russell, then aged two, was evacuated with his mother, Miriam, and his brother, from Guernsey to Stockport, Cheshire, in June 1940.

'The Germans were 30 miles away from Guernsey, in France, so Dad said we should leave and he joined the British army. We arrived in Stockport, but three weeks later Mum died of meningitis. Dad was allowed to come back to sign her death certificate, but could not look after us because he was in the forces.

'My brother and I were placed in a children's home in Styal, where we were separated. This caused me great distress, I kept asking for my Mum all the time and my brother said that I went 'berserk'. After two months, our uncle's sister-in-law in Dorset offered to take us in, but there was little affection and this had a bad effect upon me for the rest of my life.

'The Channel Islands were liberated in 1945 but it was not until 1946 that Dad came to Dorset to collect us, with a lady friend who he later married. They came in the dead of night and were strangers to us. They took us to Guernsey, where we were introduced to grandparents and aunts that we did not know. I asked Dad questions about our Mum but he had no interest in talking about her. He was also suffering from shell shock as a result of the war.

'The evacuation affected my health and education and I only discovered what real affection was when I later met my wife Paulette. We have been very happily married for years.'

Later in life Brian began to investigate his mother's death and he discovered Miriam's grave in the 1940s section of Southern Cemetery, Manchester.

Brian Russell (front left) with his mother, Miriam. (*Courtesy of Brian Russell*)

A Night of Bombing

Daniel Muir, then aged seven, was evacuated with his mother and sisters from Clydebank, Dunbartonshire, to Strone in September 1939.

Helen Muir (left) and her sister Betty and brother Daniel lost two family members during their evacuation. (*Courtesy of Dan Muir*)

'With my sisters, Betty aged nine and Helen aged five, and our mother, I was sent down river to a small town on the Firth of Clyde, called Strone. It was a great adventure for us because we had never been on holiday, and were now going by train and boat to a beautiful place, but, as we were to find out, not a welcoming one.

'We were billeted in the manse of the local church. The minister and his wife did not want us there. We stayed for three weeks then, like many other evacuees, we went home. Many evacuees returned to Clydebank, with disastrous consequences for some. We were evacuated again on Friday 14 March 1941, after a night of bombing. We had spent the previous night in a cinema, where we had gone to see a Shirley Temple film. We came out at 6am to devastation and the news that two of our uncles had been killed.

'Our house was not habitable, so we were evacuated to Helensburgh. Our father had not been at the cinema with us, and we did not know his whereabouts. We eventually ended up in a big house in Millig Street with the Snodgrass family. He was 'something in the city' [of Glasgow] so our mother became their housekeeper and we had to call the teenage sons 'Mr James' and 'Mr Gordon'. Our father eventually found us after a two-day search, but soon after was called for service in the RAF.'

Dan's family remained in Helensburgh for two years and he has mainly happy memories of this time. However, he also recalls that during this time his mother still kept hoping to see his uncles, whose bodies were never found.

Cruelty and Kindness

Jean Bell, then aged four, was evacuated from London to South Wales with her older brother and sister, in September 1939. Her younger brother joined them later.

Jean Bell (far right), pictured with her brothers and sister. (*Courtesy of Jean Bell*)

'I was picked out, with my sister, by a Welsh lady who was very cruel to us. She had a spiteful daughter who stamped on my sister's fingers when she was drawing hopscotch on the pavement. We started school without shoes and were laughed at by the local children for being badly dressed. My sister told me later that this was because our clothes had been sold. I seem to have blocked out most of what happened there, but I do know my sister was admitted to hospital with a back injury and it was at this point that we were removed from this house.

'We then lived in several different places. One lovely lady was very kind to us although soon after we moved in, I fell into the river and was too frightened to go home, as I feared being severely punished. It was dark when she found me, still very wet and scared. She took me home, gave me a big cuddle, dried me off and put me to bed. After that, I felt loved and settled down happily with her. We remained with her for a while but then, unfortunately for us, her daughter, who was in the forces, became pregnant and was sent home, so she needed our bedroom.

'In our final residence, the lady looked upon us as servants. Because I was younger I had the lightest chores, but my sister had to do the washing by hand and scrub the stone floor in the kitchen. My sister and I also ate in the kitchen, whilst the family ate in the dining room. When the war ended and we left to go home, I didn't turn round to wave goodbye to anyone.'

On their return to London the children had a medical inspection. Jean's sister had contracted TB and they were all so thin that they were allowed extra rations and received special health checks for some years.

I Wish I'd Said Goodbye

George Osborn, then aged five, and his sister Brenda, aged six, were evacuated from Portsmouth to Wootton Bridge on the Isle of Wight, in September 1939.

'My sister Brenda and I were placed in separate billets. I was badly treated in mine, but with Brenda's help, I was moved into her billet. However, on 28 December 1941 I was on my own again when Brenda died of blood poisoning. This was caused by an infection after an inoculation against diphtheria, which, ironically, was given to immunise us against a killer disease of the time.

George Osborn (right) with his sister Brenda (left), photographed on the day before they were evacuated to the Isle of Wight. (*Courtesy of George Osborn*)

'The last time I saw Brenda was some six weeks before she died, on her way to Dr. Kennedy's evening surgery, in terrible pain and with her arm swollen like a balloon. She looked back once or twice, waving in the way she always did when she was saying good-bye. I didn't bother waving back but shouted after her saying something like, "You're a cissy, it doesn't really hurt, you're only playing up."

'With all my heart I wish my last words to her had been kinder. I should have said, "Please come back soon Brenda because I shall miss you terribly. For as long as I can remember you've always been there for me; you have not only been my sister but also my best friend, mother and father, all rolled into one. I always feel safe and secure with you and you're the only person who has never let me down. It was comfortable feeling your hand in mine, even though I snatched it away when others saw me. I depend on you for so many things, so come back soon and I promise never to be spiteful or hurt you – ever again." But small brothers seldom say things like that.'

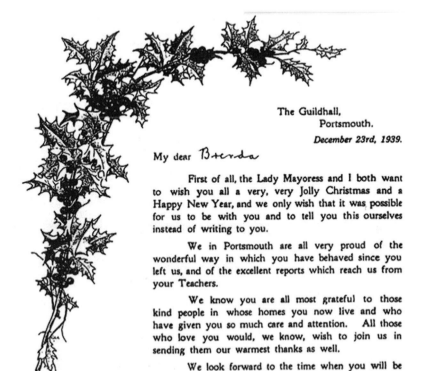

The Guildhall,
Portsmouth.

December 23rd, 1939.

My dear Brenda

First of all, the Lady Mayoress and I both want to wish you all a very, very Jolly Christmas and a Happy New Year, and we only wish that it was possible for us to be with you and to tell you this ourselves instead of writing to you.

We in Portsmouth are all very proud of the wonderful way in which you have behaved since you left us, and of the excellent reports which reach us from your Teachers.

We know you are all most grateful to those kind people in whose homes you now live and who have given you so much care and attention.   All those who love you would, we know, wish to join us in sending them our warmest thanks as well.

We look forward to the time when you will be with us again, but for the present it is much better that you should all remain where you are.

We hope that you will all keep well and happy and that this Christmas will be every bit as enjoyable as those you have had in the past.

Goodbye, and God bless you.

Yours affectionately,

Lord Mayor.

Brenda Osborn's copy of a letter from the Mayor of Portsmouth, sent out to all evacuees spending Christmas away from home. (*Courtesy of George Osborn*)

The loss of his sister helped George to be accepted in a village where newcomers would normally expect to spend two or three generations of residence, or more, before being considered to be an 'Isle of Wighter'.

A Sweet Billet

Audrey Leather, then aged five, was evacuated from Great Harwood, near Bolton, to Blackpool.

'My parents felt that I would be safer if I went to stay with my Uncle Arthur and Aunty Edith, who owned a confectionery shop just behind Blackpool Pleasure Beach. I remember leaving home with a cardboard tag with my name and a number written on it.

'I went to school in Blackpool and always got the cream from the school milk, because the 'town' kids didn't like it. Before the war, mum had delivered milk from the family farm so that's why I liked cream. The children in Blackpool used to tease me about coming from the countryside and I wasn't happy about being called an evacuee. I didn't make any real friends.

'During break and lunch times I would lock myself in the school toilets because I had chocolate biscuits and cake from Uncle's

Audrey Leather, pictured here in the 1950s, was sent to live with relatives in Blackpool. (*Courtesy of Richard Wynn*)

shop, which the other kids didn't have. I never had enough to share them round equally. However, after school, I had fun ice skating at the Pleasure Beach, going to the Fun House and eating freshly-made doughnuts.

'Polish airmen often stayed with my uncle and aunt and they were always friendly. There were times when one or more of them didn't come down to breakfast. When I asked where they were, I was told that they had 'gone home' – now I realise obviously they hadn't returned from their missions.'

Living in Blackpool changed Audrey's life, but she was glad that she hadn't been sent to live with strangers, which would have made it even more traumatic. She went to live in Uganda in the 1950s, then travelled the world, returning to visit Blackpool in the 1970s and 1980s. Audrey died in May 2005 in Zimbabwe.

Hello

How are You
My little EVACUEE?
I hope you are happy by the sea
I love your letters
Please do send another
Love and Kisses from
your MOTHER

Replica

Not all evacuees were as lucky as Audrey, but some, as this postcard shows, were billeted beside the sea. (*Author's collection*)

Nothing but Fish Paste Sandwiches

Eileen Parker, then aged nine, was evacuated with Townhill School, Swansea, to Whitland in Carmarthenshire.

'My mum just had her kidney removed, so she could not look after us, and my dad was working as a labourer for the corporation, so my brother and I were evacuated. We were sent to a farm where the people were not very nice to us.

'On the first day of school, the car we were being taken to school in crashed, though luckily we were not hurt. Every day we were given fish paste sandwiches and goat's milk, which tasted awful. My teacher saw that I was not drinking my milk. She told me to fetch it and she swapped it for her cow's milk. We could not bear the constant taste of fish paste sandwiches and had very little to eat at other times. We also had to work on the farm after school and at weekends.

'When Mum was well enough to travel, she came to visit us. As we met her on the railway station platform, she was horrified by how thin we were. She said we looked like a pair of urchins and decided to take us straight home with her, despite the dangers in Swansea. I was so relieved to be going back home! She believed that the couple who took us in only did so to get the billeting allowance.'

Eileen returned to Swansea, where she saw the High Street bombed, and a bomb go through the roof of their next-door neighbour's house. Her father was on duty as an Air Raid Precaution warden at the time.

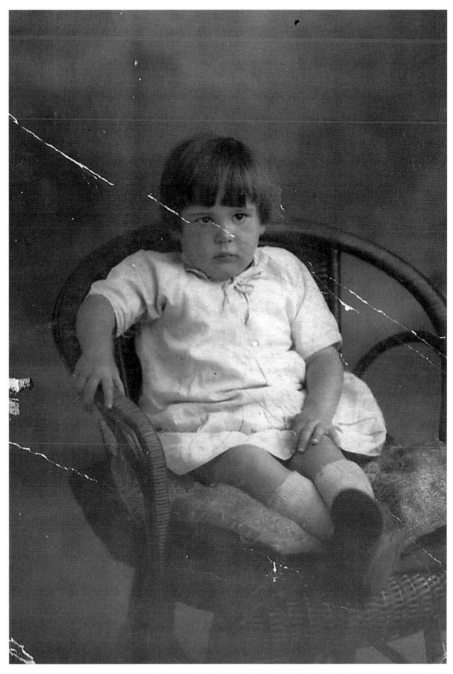

Eileen Parker was constantly hungry in her billet in Whitland. This photograph was taken several years before the war. (*Courtesy of Eileen Parker*)

Posted off Like a Parcel

Peter St John Dawe, then aged seven, was evacuated from a London orphanage to Leighton Buzzard.

Leighton Buzzard Railway Station where Peter St John Dawe spent the night alone in the station waiting room. (*Courtesy of John Alsop Collection*)

'I was evacuated after the orphanage was hit by a bomb. The surviving kids went to a convent, but nuns and children don't mix, so we were evacuated to different places. I was shipped to Leighton Buzzard by train in the guard's van like a parcel, with a label round my neck. My baggage was a paper bag with a bun, half a bar of chocolate, a three-legged piggy bank containing tuppence, and a pocket knife with a bent blade. The van was windowless, so I passed the time trying to straighten the blade of my knife against a wooden crate, but the guard stopped me. So the blade stayed bent.

'On arrival, nobody knew what to do with me. So I ate my bun and chocolate, and spent the night in the station waiting room. The next morning, I broke the piggy bank and bought a sandwich at the station buffet.

Eventually the billeting officer came, a short lady, with a short temper. She housed me temporarily with an elderly couple. That was all right, except that their house adjoined an abattoir for pigs. The squealing was terrible. From upstairs, I could see what was happening.

'Next morning, the short, short-tempered lady called. We went together to the town hall. It was market day, with pens full of sheep, cows, and pigs. One was crammed with pigs, and some men were poking them. The pigs squealed; the men laughed.

'I decided to straighten the blade of my knife under the latch. So I got to work. But I didn't expect the gate to spring open. The pigs didn't wait a second; they rushed out like demon-filled Gadarine swine. They hurtled through the market, knocking people over, and upsetting stalls. After that, I wasn't wanted in Leighton Buzzard. They hastened to get rid of me as fast and as far as possible.'

Peter was put on a train to distant Launceston. From there, he was later sent even further to a village in East Anglia.

Siblings Separated

Sheila Gibson, then aged eight, and her brother Eric, aged six, were evacuated from Castle Bromwich, Birmingham, to Hatton, near Derby, in 1940.

Sheila Gibson (standing) remained in constant touch with her foster mother, Mrs Croft (seated, centre) after the war. This photograph was taken in 2012. (*Courtesy of Sheila Gibson*)

'Unfortunately, my brother and I were separated. I was collected by Mrs Croft, who took me home to her husband, Len, and six-month-old son, Nigel. I had to get used to the countryside and the farm animals and being able to wander over the fields at the back of the house, where the River Dove ran. Over it there was a bridge leading from Hatton village to Tutbury. There is a ruined castle in Tutbury and I spent many a happy hour playing amongst the ruins.

'My brother Eric wasn't at all happy though, as he wasn't with a nice lady. He told me that in the last few months, she used to tie his hands together when he went to bed. Apparently it was to stop him scratching a sore spot on his face. Eventually he was moved but was unhappy in his next place. I met him in the village one day with his head bandaged and he told me that he had been climbing and had fallen and banged his head. The next thing I heard was that he had been taken home. He had been there 12 months, and so I was now on my own.'

Sheila returned home in September 1944, but every year she returned to visit Mr and Mrs Croft. Sheila attended Mrs Croft's hundredth birthday party in 2012. Mrs Croft passed away at the age of 101, but Sheila will always remember her with fondness.

Evacuated to a Monastery

Francis Rutter, then aged eight, was evacuated from Poplar, East London, to Redruth, Cornwall, in 1940.

'My father stubbornly refused to take shelter in the underground and died during the Blitz, so my mother decided that her children should be evacuated, while she remained in London with my baby brother.

'The train ride from London was cramped and we didn't even have access to a toilet. Some children had to wee on the floor, my sister included, as it was such a long journey. My brothers and sisters were sent to Oxford, but I was sent on to Cornwall, where I was to stay with the Benedictum Brothers. The hardest part was saying goodbye to my brothers and sisters and, being so young, I didn't understand why we couldn't all be together.

'I found it very hard to live under the Brothers' strict regime and tried on numerous occasions to run away. The only way they dealt with this was to beat me in front of the other boys at assembly, to make an example of me.

'I missed my family immensely and it still upsets me that I was sent so far away and not even to a family. I thought I would be on a farm or in the countryside, not at a strict monastery where we weren't allowed to play, or even talk most of the time.'

Francis feels that his unpleasant experience made him a stronger person. Despite her wartime sufferings, his mother lived to the age of 103.

A scene of devastation during the London Blitz. Francis Rutter lost his father during the Blitz and was evacuated to Cornwall. (*Courtesy of the New York Times Paris Bureau Collection*)

The Biscuit Tin

Faith Shoesmith, then aged six, and her sister Stella, then aged nine, were evacuated from Lowestoft to Glossop in Derbyshire.

'When we arrived, people only wanted one child. We were the last to be picked and grudgingly collected by Mrs Jessie Woods. Their daughter Rene was about 18 years old, and I don't remember her being cruel, but she was not around much. Our stay with Jessie Woods was very unhappy, as she treated us like slaves. Every Saturday we had to clean all of the bedrooms from top to bottom and we also had to polish the hall floor on our hands and knees.

'Mrs Woods inspected our work thoroughly afterwards to make sure that we had done a good job. We were not allowed into the dining room, and if we wanted to go upstairs, we had to ask permission. I would say "Please may I go upstairs?" or "Can I please go upstairs?", but it was always wrong and Mrs Woods would stand and laugh at us. We had to mind our manners, stand with straight backs and walk a certain way!

'Our dad had joined the army. Mum was in Lowestoft and every now and then she would send us parcels of sweets etc, but we never received them. She did visit us when she could, and always brought sweets and toys with her. Our one victory was that we found a large square tin of biscuits hidden behind Mrs Woods' wardrobe. Every week when we cleaned her bedroom we helped ourselves to one biscuit. After about two years Mum found a place in Sherwood and took us there so we could all be together.'

Years later, Faith and Stella discovered that Rene had written to the Lowestoft local newspaper, trying to find them. She described the two evacuees as 'poor children', which they were not. Most evacuees arrived with little clothing because there were restrictions on what they were allowed to bring. At home, Faith and Stella had some lovely dresses, as shown in the photograph above overleaf.

Faith Shoesmith (left) and her sister Stella (right) wearing dresses made by their mother in Lowestoft. (*Courtesy of Faith Catchpole, née Shoesmith*)

The Other Side of the Story

Geraldine Barker is the granddaughter of Jessie Woods, who took Faith and Stella Shoesmith, into her home.

'My late mother, Rene, upon moving to Suffolk, unsuccessfully endeavoured to contact the evacuee girls. I now understand why Faith and Stella were elusive; they had no intention of speaking to Jessie Woods' daughter. Unbelievably, my grandmother, who was always loving towards me, had been cruel to her charges.

Rene (right) had no idea of the unhappiness that Faith (left) and her sister Stella were experiencing in the family home. (*Courtesy of Geraldine Barker*)

'Yes she was rather "showy", always dressed well, and desired a home full of new things. Yes, she was self-centred and perhaps to maintain a harmonious atmosphere was indulged by my grandfather. These factors may have influenced the treatment of the evacuees, but it does not fully explain their experience.

'Jessie's father aspired to be a member of the Victorian middle class and, rising from humbler origins, would have been conscious of his achievement and social standing. My grandmother's husband, a self-employed carpenter was perhaps not socially acceptable to her parents and resulted in her efforts to keep up appearances. Moreover, the Victorian idea of self-improvement through hard work was instilled in her via the role model of her father. The toxic mix of both character and upbringing were likely to have created a narrow biased attitude towards the evacuees, indeed she considered them poor, a fact she related to my mother.

'However, there was one further twist, Jessie did not want two evacuees and this caused her resentment and inability to give comfort or love. To keep up appearances her charges needed to behave impeccably and were overworked to instil Victorian values of hard work to achieve in life.

'My dear late mother worked long hours and may have been oblivious to the evacuees' treatment. Even if she had witnessed the conduct she could not remonstrate, as my grandmother would not be criticised. I cannot provide a definitive answer. After having her own children, the plight of the evacuees would have appeared abhorrent to Mum; the thought of her own six-year-old daughter being sent away and treated so poorly would have been a burden to her. She probably wanted to say sorry to Fay and Stella on behalf of her mother.'

Waiting for Our Breakfast

Maureen Black, then aged 13, was evacuated to Hastings from St Ursula's Convent in Greenwich, London, in September 1939.

Maureen Black attended drawing lessons in the fishermen's huts at Hastings. (*Courtesy of Antony Mair, of* http://hastingspostcards.blogspot.co.uk)

'My first billet was near the High School on the Ridge and the woman took in five of us. She also took in commercial travellers, whose rooms, on the first floor, were shown to the billeting officer. Yet, she squeezed the five of us into one large attic room, and, as I was the smallest, my bed was in a cupboard on two upturned drawers with a mattress on top. Every morning we were told to wait until the commercial travellers had had their breakfast.

'We smelt the delicious bacon and eggs, but when we came downstairs we were given half a piece of bread and butter and a cup of tea. Luckily, as it was the beginning of the war, we were still able to buy chocolate. I was brought up never to tell tales and did not realise at 13 the difference between telling tales and telling what was happening.

'One of us mentioned the situation at school though, and we were moved very quickly. I went to live with a lovely family in Boyne Road, who were very kind. I also remember attending drawing lessons at the fishermen's huts in the Old Town.'

Maureen recently found a letter which she wrote to her mother from Hastings, in which she mentioned that she could hear the guns in France.

A Stony Situation

James Martin, then aged 13, was evacuated with his brothers from the East End of London to Bridgwater, Somerset, in 1939.

'The Thames shone like a silver beacon guiding German bombers to the East End. Every day we went to school prepared for possible evacuation, taking gas masks, food and belongings with us. One day we were evacuated and a neighbour told Mum who ran to the station to wave goodbye.

'We arrived in Bridgwater, where George and Frank were billeted with Arthur and Beaty Taunton at 1 Kimberley Terrace. Mum had told me to stay with my younger brother John, so we were billeted with Mr and Mrs Berry, who lived close to Kimberley Terrace. George, John and I went to Eastover School. Frank, who was the cleverest, went to a school of Engineering and Navigation, but sadly had to drop-out as our parents could not afford the uniform.

James Martin (left) and his brother Frank (right) were evacuated twice to Bridgwater in Somerset. (*Courtesy of Ursula Martin, Somerset Genealogy,* www.somersetgenealogy. uk.com)

'We stayed there for four months, then returned to London. In 1941 we returned to Bridgwater with Mum, moving into the top half of a house, whilst the resident family of Mrs Stone lived downstairs. There was tension between the families and Mrs Stone wouldn't allow us to use the downstairs bathroom whilst we were eating.

'We were eventually given a house at 6 Market Street. One of the houses had a dog kennel which was connected to the mains gas and my brother George remembers watching dogs going in and being gassed. On one occasion a poor big black dog went in, the operator closed the door and sat smoking a cigarette. He opened the door, the dog walked out and was immediately pushed back in.'

Soon after James joined the Forces in 1944, their street in London was bombed. The house didn't take a direct hit but was made unsafe, and the family remains in Bridgwater to this day.

In Search of a Place of Safety

Jean Arthur, then aged five, was evacuated from London to Cornwall in September 1939.

'My brother and I were firstly sent to Cornwall, where I was extremely unhappy. The couple who cared for us had no children and were very cold hearted. I pined so badly for Mum that I started wetting the bed. I got thrashed and each night I would get pray to God on my hands and knees, 'Please don't let me go to sleep and wet the bed', but of course I fell asleep and wet it. The husband tried to interfere with me when his wife was out. The neighbours must have realised what was going on because they complained to the authorities about our treatment.

Jean Arthur lived in constant fear of German aircraft like this one, crashing into her home in Worthing. (*Courtesy of Andrew Williamson*)

'We then moved to a family who had lots of children. However, Mum visited us and was horrified by the basic conditions – there was no proper toilet – so she took us away with her. As London was so dangerous, she found a house in Worthing, near to her sister, so we were all together again. However, it was not the safest place as there were gun emplacements on the seafront protecting supply ships. So if German aircraft crossed Worthing they were shot at and sometimes they crashed on the town.

'One day I was at school and someone came into the class and spoke quietly to my teacher, then they both looked straight at me. I thought, "Oh no, my Mum has been killed!" A German plane had crashed right into our house but luckily Mum had been out shopping at the time.'

Jean lived in several more billets where she was very unhappy. At one point, she was evacuated to Nelson in Lancashire to a lovely couple, the only kind foster parents she had during the war.

A Night in the Coal Shed

Peggy White, then aged nine and her sister Betty, then aged twelve, were evacuated from London to Oxford in September 1939.

'Our first home was with Mr and Mrs Murphy, who had the kindest faces we had ever seen. Betty and I were made welcome, even though Mr and Mrs Murphy had not long moved in and were practically still on their honeymoon. With no extra beds to be had at that time, they put the seats from the settee and armchairs on the floor and made them into comfortable beds for us and, although we were scheduled to stay for one night only, my sister stayed for two years (until she left school to start work) and I stayed for five years.

Peggy White experienced both love and cruelty in two Oxford billets. (*Courtesy of Peggy White*)

'We left "aunt" Maisie and "uncle" Charlie when Maisie was expecting her first baby and wasn't very well. We moved in with Mrs Fisher, who turned out to be the most wicked woman we had ever met. We were beaten, made to do all the housework before school, and were shut, one at a time, in a dark coal shed all night. There were huge spiders and it was bitterly cold.

'About a year later, Betty's teacher, Mrs Payne, saw the terrible bruises on her. She questioned us both, took us back to the house and told us to pack our belongings, while she had words with Mrs Fisher. As we left, Mrs Payne said "Where would you like to live most of all?" Betty and I cried in unison, "With Mrs Murphy." She replied "That's just where we are going." Mrs Murphy cried when she saw us, and so did we.'

To this day, Maisie is still 'Mum' to Peggy and Betty, and they will always remember the love and kindness that she and Charlie gave to them.

Missing – Presumed Dead!

Lorraine and Lloyd Savident, then aged twelve and nine, were evacuated from Guernsey with St Saviour's Junior School to Manchester in June 1940.

For four years, the parents of Lorraine Savident (left) and her brother Lloyd (right) thought that their children had died in an air raid. (*Courtesy of the Savident family*)

'It was a very long journey by sea and train, and we found Manchester big, noisy and frightening. We children and our teachers were taken into a big hall and during the night, the air raid warning sounded. We became separated from our school group, and spent the night in a shelter with elderly people.

'The next morning we discovered that our Guernsey school had been moved to another area without us! They assumed we had been killed in the air raid and had sent a message to our parents in Guernsey – just before the Germans invaded the island. So for four years our family thought we were both dead.

'In the meantime, we were chosen by a couple, Mr and Mrs Fitton, who lived in Hulme. They really only wanted a girl as company for their daughter Brenda, but we told them we didn't want to be separated, so they took us both. They cared for us very well but there were no cuddles. Local people were very nice to us, but it took some time to get used to the Manchester accents.

'In 1944 we were in a Manchester park helping to "dig for victory" and a young man in navy uniform approached us, saying "You are Lloyd and Lorraine aren't you?" He was our cousin and had somehow found us through the Red Cross. Now our family knew that we were alive!

We returned to Guernsey in 1945 and a lady came up to us and said, "I am your mother, these are your sisters and your brother."'

When they returned home Lorraine and Lloyd spoke English, but their father spoke only Guernsey patois, so they could not communicate properly. In addition, there was no bathroom or running water and the toilet was at the bottom of the garden, which took some getting used to.

Homesick and Neglected

Edna Dart, then aged eight, was evacuated from London to Paignton in September 1939.

Edna Dart (right) was abused at her foster home in Paignton. She is pictured here with her brother Victor (left) and Derek, her foster mother's brother (centre). (*Courtesy of Edna Dart*)

'My brother Victor was billeted elsewhere, while I was billeted with a classmate. Apart from crying every night because of homesickness, I spent my only happy time as an evacuee, on the back of a shire horse pulling a load of hay, singing 'South of the Border Down Mexico Way.'

'That was short-lived because I was soon moved on, alone this time, to a billet where I was neglected. For tea one day I was given a sandwich full of fat and a glass of lemonade with salt in it. I wasn't washed, my clothes weren't washed, and I had a bath about once a month. I was also physically and mentally abused by my foster father when he was home on leave. In those days, the authorities didn't check on the people they put you with.

'In spring 1940 my mother visited me and brought summer clothes, but, seeing the conditions I was living in, she told the authorities about my experience. They had me moved again. At my new home I was given a bath and clean clothes and there was an older evacuee there. It was much better. Eventually, though, our foster mother decided she could not keep both of us, so my mother took me back to London.'

Edna's experiences as an evacuee shaped her life, leaving her with agoraphobia and claustrophobia.

Boiled Mouse for Tea?

Rose Hawkins, then aged eight, was evacuated from Birmingham to Aston Ingham, Herefordshire, in September 1940.

'My brother Bill was badly injured when the factory he worked in was bombed, so Mum sent my brother John and I to the countryside. We moved in with a husband and wife who had no family, and no intention of sparing the rod or making allowances.

'Everything was regimented, our letters sent home were censored, or destroyed if they contained requests of "Please can we come home?" We walked two and a half miles each way to school and if we were late back, there was no meal, we were sent straight to bed. When I first arrived I wet the bed, as I was so scared. The woman told me, "If you wet the bed again, I will boil a mouse and make you drink the liquid!" So whenever I ate and drank anything after that, I always checked it for pieces of mouse.

Rose Hawkins (as a baby) with her sister Mabel (left), brother Bill (back right) and brother John (front right) in Birmingham. (*Courtesy of Rose Gillett, née Hawkins*)

'If her sister visited from the Isle of Wight we were sent to stay with another elderly couple in the village, sleeping with fleas and mothballs for good measure. No one to complain to. After 15 months of severe discipline, continued homesickness and begging letters home, we came back to Birmingham. It was like Christmas to us, despite the war-torn Blitz and sleepless nights in the Anderson shelter.'

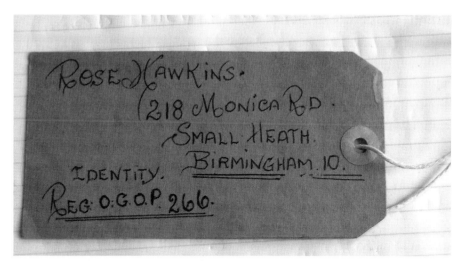

Rose Hawkins' evacuee label. (*Courtesy of Rose Gillett, née Hawkins*)

Fifty years later, Aston Ingham's evacuees held their first reunion, presenting the village with a biblical picture with this inscription 'Suffer the little children to come unto me, and forbid them not, for such is the Kingdom of Heaven.'

A Narrow Escape

Eight-year-old Ben Halligan was evacuated from Liverpool to Tetchill, Shropshire, in September 1939.

Ben Halligan (seated on the step, wearing braces) with members of his family in Liverpool. (*Courtesy of Stephen Halligan*)

'My sisters were taken away, whilst my brother and I were taken by a farmer. Two days later we were placed with a Mr and Mrs Roberts. I did not know it then but that was the luckiest day of my life. They were over the age limit for taking evacuees but when Mrs Roberts heard where we had been billeted, she insisted on taking us in.

'Six months later that farmer was arrested for strangling his wife. Mrs Roberts must have seen something in his character. There was an aura about her, when she looked into your eyes she looked into your very soul, there was no way you could tell her a lie.

'One day we were swimming in the canal and a bomber crashed, missing us by a few feet. We got the rear gunner out, who managed to limp around to help us get the other six out. One of the first we got out had half of his face crushed in but was still conscious. Some were dead but we managed to get them all out and made them as comfortable as possible. Then the police, fire and ambulance arrived. A police officer said to us, "Come on you kids, get away from here, it is no place for you." The rear gunner said to him "You leave them children alone, who do you think got all these men out of this wreckage? Instead of chasing them, you should be recommending them for medals.""

Ben has now passed away, but his family have these tales to help remember him and what he went through growing up as an evacuee.

A Journey Across the Moors

Robert Gunn, then aged 12, and his brother Ronald, then aged 10, were evacuated from Brighton to Slaithwaite in Yorkshire in 1941.

Robert Gunn (centre front) with the Downs family. (*Courtesy of Robert Gunn*)

'My new foster parents, the Downs, selected me but Ronald was taken to a place near Halifax. His foster parents were very strict. On the day I arrived, Mr Downs took me to buy a new bed in Huddersfield. Unbeknown to him I was suffering from diarrhoea, from the soup-type meal we had on the train, and he knocked on someone's door to ask if I could use the toilet. With no hesitation, they said yes – a sign of the sort of close community I had arrived in. Opposite the Downs' house was a butcher who raised chickens on agricultural land. I was paid to feed them with buckets of corn seed which I scattered over the fields.

'One day there was a knock on our door and there were two carer people holding my brother and another boy. Ronald had decided to come and find me and they'd walked 10–12 miles over the moor until they found Slaithwaite. The Downs invited them in for tea and they stayed for an hour. The Downs told my mother that Ronald had walked over the moors to see me. She wrote back, saying that she was coming to see me and would then take me to see my brother at his foster address.

'I accumulated a large tin of sweets from my pocket money to take to my brother. Me and my mother travelled to Halifax (I tripped and spilled the sweets all over the floor of the bus, but picked them up again). When we arrived, mother sent us out to play while she talked to my brother's foster parents. When we returned, mother had decided to bring us both back to Brighton and Ronald's bags were packed. We returned to Slaithwaite and stopped overnight.'

The next day Robert, Ronald and his mother made their way back to Brighton. His mother said, "If we're going to die, we'll die together."

Women's Voluntary Service recruitment poster. (*Author's collection*)

Chapter Five

'We Were With the Children': Organising Evacuation

Guernsey evacuees thank British towns and cities for caring for evacuees, on Liberation Day, 9 May 1946. (*Courtesy of The Carel Toms Collection, Guernsey*)

These stories pay tribute to the adults who were involved in the evacuation and care of millions of children. They include the accounts of mothers, teachers, nursing staff, billeting officers and liaison officers. They also mention the efforts of the Women's Voluntary Service (WVS), which provided invaluable assistance to evacuees during the war.

This chapter also recognises thousands of teachers who accompanied their pupils in September 1939, leaving their own families behind. In many cases teachers took responsibility for these children for years, 24 hours a day, seven days a week. Once settled in the reception areas, they supervised not only the education of the children, but their health, safety and welfare.

One girl understood their sacrifice only too well. Just a few years after being evacuated as a 15-year-old, she became a student teacher and was put in charge of a group of evacuees.

Thousands of mothers also travelled with evacuated schools as helpers. In some cases they returned home within a week or two, but others remained in the reception areas and helped to care for the pupils, providing a link with home. In addition, pregnant women were encouraged to move to safer areas. Whole families often fled to safety in the countryside, while others left war-torn Europe for the comparative safety of the British mainland.

Many of the evacuees I have interviewed say that they will never forget the kindness of the volunteers who greeted them as they arrived – especially the WVS and the Salvation Army. They also remember the officials who helped ease their way into a new life in an unfamiliar part of the country. A file in Bury Archives contains post-war thank-you letters sent to the billeting officer, Miss Roberts, from thankful mothers who had been evacuated to Bury from Guernsey.

An Invitation to the White House

Paulette Le Mescam, then aged eight, was sent from Paris to Guernsey, then evacuated with her Guernsey school to Knutsford, Cheshire, in June 1940.

'When my mother died, father sent me to live with my grandmother in Guernsey. However, when Guernsey was under threat of German invasion, the Guernsey schools were evacuated. My school, together with Father Bleach and some of the nuns, arrived in Knutsford where we were given permission to operate as a Guernsey school.

'We moved into an empty mansion, but Father Bleach had no money to feed and clothe any of us or buy school books and equipment. He found out about the Foster Parent Plan for War Children and each child in my school was sponsored by a kind American. My sponsor was a lady I knew as "Aunty Eleanor", who sent money, exchanged letters with me and sent me lovely parcels.

Paulette Le Mescam (centre, holding toy bus) made an unusual friend during wartime. (*Author's collection*)

'Later I discovered that Aunty Eleanor was Mrs Eleanor Roosevelt, the wife of the American President! I spoke on BBC radio about her and reporters came to our school to take photographs. In May 1945 Guernsey was liberated, so we prepared to return home. Aunty Eleanor invited me to visit the White House but I was without the means to do this.'

When Paulette returned to Guernsey, her grandmother had died and she was sent to live with an uncle that she did not know. She never saw her father again. Looking back, Paulette recalls that it was wonderful to receive letters and parcels from someone who cared about her.

Taking Cover in the Caves

Pam Davey, then aged seven, and her family were evacuated from West Wickham, Kent to the Chislehurst Caves in September 1940.

Pam Davey (front row, fourth from the left) spent part of the war living in a cave. (*Courtesy of Jim Davey*)

'I wonder how many readers have lived in a cave. My family fled our home because of constant bombing and went to live in Chislehurst Caves for a year or more. We slept in bunk beds and I remember that the water was chalky. My mother used to queue up for a teapot of tea and she heated baked beans and other things on a primus stove. We children used to go to concerts inside. We put a row of flowers to show where the stage was.

'At the height of the bombing, up to 15,000 people lived in the caves, and the Government eventually installed canteens, sanitary, hospital and washing facilities. Over the years church services and entertainments, such as dances and film shows, were held. You can still visit the caves. Some time in 1941/42 we were evacuated to Longsight, Manchester. We were all split up until my father found a house and came to collect us.'

Pam's family later returned to London, just as the V2 rockets began to arrive. Pam passed away in August 2013.

Evacuated as a Mother-to-be

Mrs Jessie Braisted was evacuated from London to Loughborough in spring 1943.

'Because I was pregnant, it was decided that I should be evacuated. It was a strange experience leaving my home and family in Greenwich. I travelled to Loughborough with other pregnant women by train, under the supervision of the WVS (Women's Voluntary Service).

Jessie Braisted gave birth to her son, Ian, during her evacuation in Loughborough. (*Courtesy of the Braisted family*)

'We met the host families in a village hall and I was allocated to a home owned by a young couple with a little girl who was around two years old; they called her 'Tiny' because she was delicate, and I remember the family being worried about their daughter's health. I did all I could to help with the family chores. I would take Tiny to the park and would often meet up with other evacuee to-be-mums. The man of the house worked in a factory called the 'Brush' and there was one air-raid during the time I stayed with the family.

'When I went into labour, the family contacted the WVS, who escorted me to Long Whatton House. I had a long labour and my son, Ian, was born on 17 June 1943. I stayed on for two weeks and my mother came to visit me, but because of work commitments my husband kept in contact by letter and sent parcels.

'When the big day arrived to return home I travelled with a group of new mothers and their babies. Back in London I celebrated the birth of my baby with family members, and wrote a long letter to my host family thanking them for their wonderful hospitality.'

Jessie corresponded for a time with her host family but eventually lost touch. She thinks that they may have lived on Park Drive and that there is a 'bird' name either in the name of the road or that of the host family. Sadly, Jessie's son, Ian, passed away in February 2014.

Escaping to England

Frederick W Veale, then aged 31, was a Liaison Officer to 17,000 Guernsey evacuees who fled to England in June 1940, just days before their island was occupied by Germany.

'Whilst the evacuation was proceeding, very little was known in Guernsey of the final destination of the refugees in England. I was selected as one of three Liaison Officers who would deal with matters between the English and Guernsey authorities. We left Guernsey on 22 June and were received with courtesy in Weymouth, but found that most of the refugees had moved on from Weymouth, with others volunteering to join HM Forces. We were advised that care had been taken to place food and water on all the trains.

Frederick Veale helped thousands of fellow Guernsey evacuees to deal with the authorities in England and Scotland. (*Courtesy of Mr John Veale*)

'We left Weymouth on 25 June and proceeded to Manchester, Leeds, Edinburgh and Glasgow where we made contact with the Ministry of Health Officers. We also visited our refugees, who were mostly placed in church halls and other buildings taken over for the purpose. In some areas the officials were working closely to the Ministry's instructions for dealing with 'foreign war refugees', and restrictions, which were designed to deal with groups of aliens, caused some friction between the officials and the islanders, who are of course, British subjects. In some areas, it was possible to place the evacuated Guernsey schools in empty buildings, so that teachers and pupils could remain together in England.'

Frederick later discovered that, during the long train journeys from Weymouth, many evacuees had travelled long distances without refreshments, and that some were actually locked in trains without sanitary conveniences. They had arrived at their destinations in a distressed condition.

The Weekly Cake

Ken Chamberlain, then aged nine, was evacuated from Liverpool to Eccleston, near St Helens, Lancashire, in 1941. He was later joined by the rest of his family.

'I was sent to live with my Auntie Dolly, Uncle George and cousin Joyce in Howards Lane. It was difficult moving from an area I knew well, where I had lots of friends, to a place where I knew no-one. Everyone had a totally different accent to mine, so there was a certain amount of bullying by some children until another Liverpool boy came to live in the village and took my side.

'Later, my mother, father and younger brother Norman left Liverpool and moved into my Gran's house, at 7 Sadlers Lane, where I joined them. There were no trams or buses, so we walked four miles to school every day, along the East Lancs Road, down Houghtons Lane in all weathers – in the winter the snow could drift quite deep.

After being evacuated alone, Ken Chamberlain was reunited with members of his family (above) at 7 Sadlers Lane, Eccleston. (*Courtesy of Ken Chamberlain*)

'We were fortunate that Grandad had quite a number of hens, so eggs were available, as well as the occasional chicken. Rabbits were in abundance and my mother and grandmother were capable of turning out rabbit pies. My grandmother brought her experience forward from having to feed shooting parties when they lived at Brandreth House. One of the days to look forward to was the day that Seddons arrived with their van. This contained bread, but also trays of cakes. Norman and I were allowed to choose just one, and this was to be our treat for the week.'

The family returned to Liverpool in 1944. Ken realises that Eccleston played an important part in his life and feels that in such situations 'there are always some negatives, some major some minor, but one has to get on and cope.'

'My Micky'

Mabel Steer, in Bideford, Devon, cared for Micky Archer, then aged seven, an evacuee from Bristol. Mabel's granddaughter, Val Morrish, shares the story.

'When Micky arrived at Bideford Railway Station he had already been allocated to a local business family, but because of the colour of his skin they felt unable to take him. My Gran, Mabel Steer, had lost two of her four brothers in the First World War and was on her own. She immediately stepped in and said she would be happy to have him. She grew to love him dearly and always referred to him as 'my Micky'. I am given to understand that he was the only coloured child at that time in Bideford. I am extremely proud of my Gran, as she did recount a few times that there was some surprise at her taking the little boy into her home.'

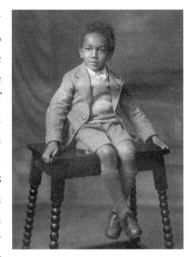

Mabel Steere took Micky Archer (above) into her home. (*Courtesy of Val Morrish*)

Micky remained in contact with Mabel until she died. Clearly, there was a very strong bond between them.

From Evacuee to Foster-Family

Norah Cheel, then aged nine, was evacuated from London to Castle Ashby, Northampton, in September 1939.

'The family were very kind to me, they had a nice garden and their little house was on the village green, next to the Post Office and the village smithy. Unfortunately after about 12 months they had to return to their home in Scotland, and a new billet had to be found for me.

'The billeting officer asked me if I would like to live with his family instead. He and his wife were also from Scotland. I stayed with them and loved being there. They had a good library, which I was allowed to use. She taught me how to manage in the kitchen

Norah Cheel (on the right) found happiness with her foster mother (rear of photograph) in Castle Ashby. (*Courtesy of Norah Killingbeck, née Cheel*)

and when they had visitors I was made to feel part of the household.

'However, when the Blitz was at its worse in London, my father decided to send all the womenfolk in our family to Castle Ashby, so that he could get on with his work without worrying every time there was an air raid. They arrived: my grandmother, her three daughters, my cousin, my sister and two dogs, Sally and Jill. They stayed at the local inn, until Lord Northampton could find accommodation for them, and I then joined them. My grandmother and aunt wanted to help the war effort, so they looked after at least 12 children from London who had been orphaned.'

Whenever Norah returns to Castle Ashby she feels as if she has come home.

Evacuated to Take Exams

Brenda Harley, then aged 15, was evacuated from Ilford to Aberdare in September 1939.

'I was 15 years old when I became an evacuee. When war was declared my family were returning to Ilford, after an idyllic holiday in the Lake District. Without daily newspapers and radio we had had no idea of the imminence of war.

'My school had already been evacuated to Ipswich and, because I wanted to become a teacher, I knew that I had to stay on at school. On 4 September I left my family for Ipswich, but in 1940 our school was moved to Aberdare, South Wales. They were expecting 5 to 11 year olds and no one wanted a strapping young lady like me. I think they felt that I would eat too much of their food!

'Eventually Mrs Davies agreed to take me on. This was a miner's household, with no bathroom, an outside toilet and a tin bath in

Brenda Harley (centre) was evacuated with her school, but in 1944 she took a party of school children to safety in Mansfield. (*Courtesy of Brenda Jenkins, née Harley*)

front of the kitchen fire (a culture shock). They were a kindly, welcoming family and in time I learned to read and pronounce Welsh by singing hymns in Gadlys Chapel. Schooling was half-day sharing with the girls' grammar school and literally any space available was used for lessons. I had exams to prepare for – my French oral exam was on 31 May and the books arrived on 29 May!

'For two years we attended summer 'Farm War Work' weeks. Nina Mabey, the future writer Nina Bawden (author of *Carrie's War*), kept us all highly entertained with a story about Herbertina the cow which lived under my bed (at the time I had a massive crush on a local Welsh lad called Herbert).'

In 1942 Brenda left school in Aberdare to train as a teacher in Saffron Walden, and in 1944 she was evacuated to Mansfield in charge of 11 primary school children.

"Can you run?"

Miss Grace Fry, a teacher, left Guernsey with pupils from the Vauvert School, arriving in Weymouth in June 1940.

'As an air raid began my group and I were pushed out of the building onto a bus. Then, to my horror, the driver locked the door and disappeared. The children had been sick on the boat and were dropping off the bus seats in the dark because they were tired. After an hour, I had given up and thought, 'Well, this is the end, if a bomb falls on us, I hope it happens quickly!' Then the driver unlocked the door and said "Out!" I had to feel with my foot under the seats in the dark to check whether I had all the children or not.

Guernsey teachers, mothers and children arriving in Cheshire in Summer 1940. (*Courtesy of Mrs R. Hammarskjold*)

'We were then sent to the railway station. Young soldiers began to push the children onto a train, then suddenly this big major came out of the darkness, and said, "Madam will you go on with your children?!" I said "But where?" Well, the train started to move, and a young lieutenant came running down the platform, grabbed my hand and said "Can you run?" and we set off at a terrific lick! A steward appeared in a white coat, at the open train door, and this young soldier pushed me into his arms, and then off we went.'

Having barely managed to board the train, Grace and her pupils were sent to Pollokshields, Glasgow.

The Evacuees Who Made Her Smile

Linda Mitchelmore's mother, Bessie Giles, lived in Wales, and looked after Kathleen and Marina Skelton, who were evacuated from Deal, Kent.

'My mother, Bessie, was always a rather stern woman who showed little affection, and I have no photographs of her smiling. Yet, in all the photographs taken of her with the evacuees, she is smiling and she looked after them wonderfully.

'She was a skilled dressmaker, her grandfather had been a tailor and taught her all the skills. She made lovely coats and clothes for the girls, even though their own mother could have afforded to buy them clothes. Mrs Skelton came to visit them now and again, by car, at my mother's home in Park Terrace, Sarn, near Bridgend. My mother told me that Kathleen and Marina were very bright academically too.'

Bessie Giles (right) could not help but smile whenever she was in the company of evacuee Marina Skelton (left). (*Courtesy of Linda Mitchelmore*)

Bessie must have cared very much for Kathleen and Marina because she carried their photographs around with her all her life, through eight house moves.

A Warm Welcome to Kent

Mary Richardson, then aged 23, was a teacher in charge of children evacuated from Cork Street School, Camberwell, to Brasted, Kent, in September 1939.

'Each teacher was assigned 10 children and we walked to Loughborough Junction Station, with mothers lining the pavements, crying and waving. We arrived at Sevenoaks, where we were neatly put into cattle pens to be counted. We caught another train and arrived at Brasted Station, which is quite a distance from the village, so when we arrived at the church hall we were a sorry sight – tired, thirsty and afraid.

Mary Richardson, a teacher from London, praised the people of Brasted for the kindness they showed to her pupils. (*Courtesy of Margaret Brown*)

'Mothers came and chose us and I was seized upon by the lady at the village shop and bakehouse. We had promised to try to keep families together, but with four Peabody girls and four Sparrowhawk boys, this proved impossible. By morning we were met with distraught mothers. Most of the younger children had head lice, some had wet their beds, and their clothing was dirty, ragged and unsuitable.

'The Kentish mothers were brilliant, extra clothing was found, menus were changed to accommodate townies who never ate greens, cuddly toys were given to comfort the weepy ones and we teachers set about de-lousing. We walked along the lovely country lanes and few Camberwell children had ever picked blackberries or seen a cow, sheep or pig. Because of transport difficulties, few London mothers came to Brasted, but the children grew strong and rosy-cheeked due to the love and care they received.'

Mary moved to a teaching job in York in October 1940, just as evacuees from Bermondsey were arriving there. The children settled well, but the mothers (who had thought they were going to Blackpool), resented 'being dumped miles from anywhere, no shops, no buses, not anything.'

Moving around Manchester

Evelyn May Brouard, then aged 28, was evacuated from Guernsey to Manchester with her 14-month-old son Ivan, in June 1940. She was pregnant with her son Michael, who was born in Manchester.

'Firstly, we were sent to an evacuee reception centre at Thame Street, Manchester, then billeted with a Mrs Williamson. We were then billeted with a Mrs Baker, but she wanted to take in some airmen instead, so we shared a house with another Guernsey lady, Lizzie Guille. I had my own room but we shared the rest of the house. It was so very different in Manchester compared to Guernsey, as there were lots of houses, all looking the same, in long rows. It was dirty there, all smoke and soot, and your washing got black when you hung it out to dry.

'We had an air raid shelter in the garden but we always went under the stairs, in the cellar. I would have preferred to use the shelter, it was brick and above ground. On one occasion, a bomb fell two rows of houses away, and we heard it fall. Later we went to have a look at the damage and there was a car on the second floor of the houses, it had been blasted up there by the bomb!

'We didn't mix much with local people, usually only at the shops. Three Guernsey families lived on our street and we met Guernsey people at a few of the Channel Island Society meetings. We spoke Guernsey patois in the house. The children spoke mostly English, which they picked up when they went to school.'

Evelyn, Michael and Ivan returned to Guernsey in October 1945, only to discover that their home had been demolished by the Germans. Michael met his father, Wilfred, who had remained in Guernsey for the duration of the war, for the first time.

Evelyn Brouard (left) left Guernsey with her son Ivan (right) and gave birth to Michael (centre) in Manchester soon after. (*Courtesy of the estate of Evelyn Brouard*)

No More School Holidays

Ben Howard, then aged 12, was evacuated with Catford Central School, London, to Sayers Croft Camp, near Cranleigh, Surrey, in May 1940.

Sayers Croft Camp became home to the boys of Catford Central School during the war. (*Courtesy of Ben Howard*)

'Two hundred of us, with our teachers, arrived at the camp which consisted of 14 buildings. Five dormitories with adjacent toilet blocks, a school block with four classrooms, a craft block, assembly hall and a dining hall. The camp was staffed mainly by local people and there was a group of housemaids from Wales, but not many male staff. Two sewing maids took care of torn shirts and holes in socks. Sometimes a barber visited, but not as as frequently as the headmaster would have liked.

'Our teachers were presented with a serious problem. They were now responsible for schoolboys 24 hours a day and none of them had boarding school experience. There would be no school holidays. After discussion it was agreed that every teacher would be on duty for 11 days out of 14. There would be some sessions off during that time but they would have to remain in camp.

'The health of the boys and staff was looked after by two nursing sisters. They had a 'sick bay' with six beds and a daily clinic for minor problems. There were occasional outbreaks of child diseases like scarlet fever and measles. Ironically, the healthiest dormitory with the least illness, was right next to the camp sewage disposal unit!'

Two murals were painted in the Sayers Camp dining hall by the pupils. They depicted winter activities and summer activities and are now registered as war memorials. Ben recalls how much of the teaching took place outside: games, football, cricket, long walks and nature studies. It was a really good evacuation as far as he was concerned.

I Wanted to Adopt my Evacuee!

Edith Ashmall lived in Rolleston-on-Dove, Staffordshire, and looked after Douglas Wood, who had been evacuated from Birmingham.

'Douglas was only five when he came to me and, at the time, he had only been at school for one week. He was such a nice boy and never any trouble to me. Even then he had something 'special' about him and we were like 'mother and son'. During the war I asked his parents if I could adopt him, but sadly they refused.'

Douglas Wood in Edith Ashmall's garden. Their wartime bond was so strong that Edith wished to adopt him. (*Courtesy of Douglas Wood*)

From the moment he returned home to Birmingham, Edith remained in touch with Douglas until she passed away in 1989. Douglas's own story is included in this book.

Finding Ourselves to be 'Foreigners'

Mrs Agnes Camp was pregnant when she fled Guernsey to England with her son Dennis, aged four, in June 1940.

'The ship took a long time to get to Weymouth because it had to avoid all the mines laid in the Channel. We disembarked in the pouring rain and I was ready for a nice cup of tea, but firstly we had our heads examined for lice and nits, which we found very embarrassing.

'We boarded a train and as we went along people threw parcels of food through the open windows and we were very grateful for their generosity. We arrived in Yorkshire, where kind people had prepared a nice buffet for us and lots of cups of tea. Dennis wasn't very well and I was quite worried. We spent the night on camp beds with an army blanket to cover us.

When Agnes Camp arrived in England from Guernsey, people were amazed that she could speak English. (*Courtesy of Karen Frith*)

'The next day we were taken to our billets. The northern people knew very little about the Channel Islands and thought we were all going to be 'black people', so they were also amazed that we could speak English. I phoned my husband in Guernsey and told him that we were safe, gave him our number and asked him to phone me the next day. That call never came because the Germans invaded Guernsey and all communications were cut. Dennis then came down with pneumonia and nearly died.'

Agnes eventually moved into a house in Stockport with her sister, and worked as a 'clippie' (ticket collector) on the trams. One day Agnes was walking home, pushing her baby daughter in her pram when a German plane flew overhead and started shooting. She managed to get the pram into the house in the nick of time. Her son Dennis's story is included in this book.

From Belgium to the Blitz

Marie Cappart's grandparents, Louis and Suzanne Nicholls, fled Belgium to England on 17 May 1940.

'My British granddad (born to a Belgian mother) fled Belgium with his wife, Suzanne, two young children, his parents and several other relatives. My great-aunt Lucie's diary states that they crossed the French border, where they were 'living like bohemians … who would have thought 15 days ago that we would starve and beg for a piece of bread?' On 24 May they witnessed a baby die of starvation.

'The Channel crossing was chaotic and the family were sent to London, where they experienced the Blitz. They later moved to the Hereford countryside, where granddad served with the RAF as a technical engineer. Grandmother was really homesick, but she said that the village people were really good to her, bringing milk, eggs and food supplies. My mother was born during this time, and my uncles, André and Jean Pierre went to school. Meanwhile my great-grandparents, Ernest Frank and Marie Louise, went to stay with relatives in Derbyshire. Ernest had been born there and he was too old to serve in the forces.

Louis Nicholls (pictured, front as a child with his parents and sister) brought his family to London from Belgium in 1940. (*Courtesy of Marie Cappart*)

'The family (apart from Marie Louise) returned to Belgium in 1946. They stayed with my grandmother's family, then the council found a small house for them. From that day on, my family were known as 'les anglais' (the English), even though they had lived in Belgium before the war! My granddad often spoke of going back to live in England but this never happened.'

Marie Louise Nicholls died in 1941 and was buried in Spital Cemetery, Chesterfield, Derbyshire. Marie hopes that one day she will visit to place flowers on her great-grandmother's grave.

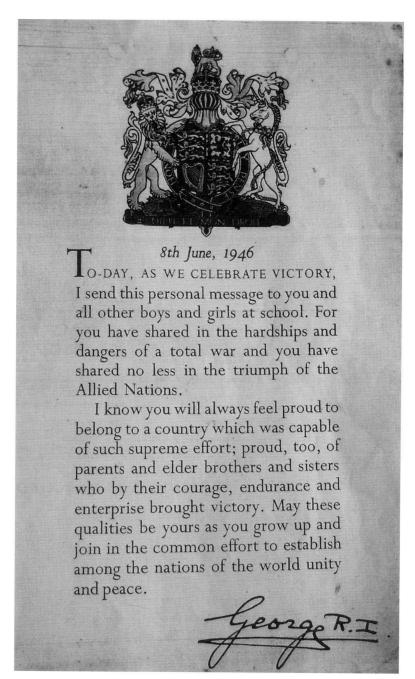

8th June, 1946

TO-DAY, AS WE CELEBRATE VICTORY, I send this personal message to you and all other boys and girls at school. For you have shared in the hardships and dangers of a total war and you have shared no less in the triumph of the Allied Nations.

I know you will always feel proud to belong to a country which was capable of such supreme effort; proud, too, of parents and elder brothers and sisters who by their courage, endurance and enterprise brought victory. May these qualities be yours as you grow up and join in the common effort to establish among the nations of the world unity and peace.

George R.I

Letter sent by the King in 1946 to British children. (*Courtesy of Rose Gillett, née Hawkins*)

Acknowledgements

Front cover upper image of evacuated children from the Channel Islands arriving in Bolton, 1940. (*courtesy of the Bolton News*).

Front cover lower image of evacuated children arriving in Bingham, 1940, reproduced courtesy of the *Nottingham Evening Post* and Picture the Past (*www.picturethepast.org.uk*).

Chapter One

Peter Campbell's story is reproduced courtesy of Peter Campbell, (see *www. leshaigh.co.uk/folkestone/evacuee.html*).

Kurt Gutmann's story is reproduced courtesy of Rod Edgar, Chief Reporter, Dumfriesshire Newspapers Group and The Devil's Porridge Museum, Annan.

Ralf Risk's interview was undertaken by John McGee of Wheech Scottish Ancestry Services.

Chapter Two

James Brown's story is reproduced courtesy of Mackenzie Brown.

Clifford Broughton's story is reproduced courtesy of People of Cwmamman website (*www.cwmammanhistory.co.uk*).

William Flynn's story is reproduced courtesy of Mackenzie Brown.

Anthony Richards' story is reproduced courtesy of Stillington and District Community Archive (*www.stillingtoncommunityarchive.org*).

Chapter Three

Harry Flack's story is reproduced courtesy of the Petrockstowe website *http://petrockstowevillage.co.uk*

Pierre Ratcliffe's story is reproduced courtesy of the HMS *Venomous* website: *www.holywellhousepublishing.co.uk / Ratcliffe.html*

Chapter Four

Maureen Black's story is reproduced courtesy of Nathan Goodwin, from his book Hastings Wartime Memories and Photographs (Phillimore, 2011).

James Martin's story is reproduced courtesy of Ursula Martin, Somerset Genealogy *www.somersetgenealogy.uk.com*

Peter St John Dawe's books on children's gangs during the Second World War are based on his own evacuation experiences, which you can read more about on his website, *www.peterstjohn.net*

Chapter Five

'We Were With the Children': Organising evacuation

Frederick W. Veale's story is reproduced courtesy of Mr John Veale.

Grace Fry's interview is reproduced courtesy of the Guernsey Retired Teachers Association.

Bibliography

Lois M. Ainger, *My Case Unpacked*, (Lois M Ainger, 1995).

Jessica Axford, (née Young), *I lived in a Castle*, (Antony Rowe, 1994).

Christopher J. Brooks, *When will I see you again? The story of East coast evacuees*, (Rushmere, 1991).

Mackenzie Brown, *Annies War*, (Mack Brown Books, via Createspace, 2014).

Mike England, *A Victorian Family at Llanhydrock* (Bodmin Books, 2001).

Lourdes Galliano, *A Rocky Passage to Exile; The war memoirs of a Gibraltarian child evacuee 1940-1945*, (Self-published, copies available from *maggie_ galliano@hotmail.com*).

Nathan Goodwin, *Hastings Wartime Memories and Photographs*, (Phillimore & Co Ltd, 2011).

Pam Hobbs, *Don't Forget to Write: The true story of an evacuee and her family*, (Ebury Press, 2009).

Hilda Hollingsworth, *They Tied a Label on my Coat*, (Virago, 1991).

Neil Holmes, *Liverpool Blitzed: Seventy Years On*, (Halsgrove, 2011).

Ben Howard, *From Brown Hill to Pitch Hill: The wartime history of two Catford schools*, (Sayers Croft War Memorials Preservation Fund).

B. S. Johnson (ed.), *The Evacuees*, (Victor Gollancz, 1968).

Audrey Jones, *Farewell Manchester: The story of the 1939 Evacuation* (Didsbury Press, 1989).

Daniel Kirmatzis, *The Biggest Scrum that Ever Was': A history of Emanuel School at War* (Troubador/Matador Press, 2014)

Nick Le Poidevin, *Torteval School in Exile*, (ELSP, 2010).

Gillian Mawson , *Guernsey evacuees: The Forgotten Evacuees of the Second World War*, (History Press, 2012).

Gillian Mawson, 'Guernsey Mothers and their Children: Forgotten Evacuees' in Professor Maggie Andrews and Dr Janis Lomas (eds) *The*

Home Front in Britain: Images, Myths and Forgotten Experiences 1914-2014, (Palgrave Macmillan, 2014).

Jean C. Noble, *Golden Girls and Downham Days*, (J C Noble, 1999).

Olive Quin, *The Long Goodbye: A Guernsey woman's story of the evacuation years*, (Guernsey Press, 1985).

Brian Ahier Read, *No Cause for Panic: Channel Island Refugees 1940-1945* (Seaflower Books, 1995).

Rita Roberts, *Toffee Apples and Togas*, (Spiderwize, 2011).

James Roffey, *Send Them to Safety: A Story of the Great British Evacuation of the Second World War*, (Evacuee Reunion Association, 2009).

Julie Summers, *When the Children Came Home: Stories of wartime evacuees*, (Simon and Schuster, 2011).

Peter Tab (ed.) *Jersey Evacuees Remember*, (The Jersey Evacuees Association, 2011).

R. Titmuss *Problems of Social Policy*, (HMSO, 1959).

Lorne A. Wallace (ed.) *Here Come the Glasgow Keelies!* (Dunning Parish Historical Society, 1999).

John Welshman, *Churchill's Children: The Evacuee Experience in Wartime Britain*, (Oxford University Press, 2010).

Sue Wheatcroft, *Worth Saving: Disabled Children during the Second World War*, (Manchester University Press, 2013).

Websites on Evacuation

Bideford 500 Heritage: *www.bidefordheritage.co.uk/htdocs/evacuees.htm*
The site celebrates Bideford's unique past and includes a number of stories related to wartime evacuation in Bideford.

Gillian Mawson: Guernsey Evacuation blog: *http://guernseyevacuees. wordpress.com*
The site gives up to date information on my ongoing research into the Guernsey Evacuation. It includes details of my talks, and of the activities of my community group of evacuees. There is also a page which shows requests from evacuees who wish to be reunited with wartime friends.

Gillian Mawson's History blog: *http://whaleybridgewriter.blogspot.co.uk*
The site contains posts on various subjects, including the Great War, the Second World War, local history and family history.

Memories of War: *www.memoriesofwar.org.uk*

The Memories of War project focusses on the oral histories of people who witnessed and experienced very different aspects of war.

Picture the Past: *www.picturethepast.org.uk*
The site contains over 100,000 fully searchable images on how life has changed in the North East Midlands over the last few hundred years

The Second World War Experience Centre: *www.war-experience.org*

The centre collects and encourages access to the testimony of men and women who lived through the Second World War. This ensures that different audiences share and learn from the personal recollections preserved in the collection.

The Evacuees Reunion Association

The Evacuees Reunion Association (ERA) was formed in 1995 to ensure that the true story of the great evacuation would become better known and preserved for future generations. Founded by a former evacuee, James Roffey, the ERA is a registered charity, managed by former evacuees and others interested in the subject.

It aims to place on record the impact that the evacuation had upon communities throughout the United Kingdom, not just those in the departure areas, but also those in the designated reception areas. The story of the evacuation has been surrounded by wildly believed myths ever since the scheme was first suggested by the British government. The true story has so many different facets, covering every aspect of the long term effects that evacuation had upon the individuals and communities that were involved.

Every day the ERA receives the true stories of former evacuees. They vary from idyllic to accounts of great hardship and privation. It also records the stories of the evacuation of children from the homeland to Canada, Australia, New Zealand and South Africa. Operated by the Children's Overseas Reception Board, it was a scheme that was brought to an abrupt and tragic end by enemy action.

The association organises reunion meetings and publishes a monthly newsletter, entitled *The Evacuee,* which is sent free to ERA members. The 'Lost Touch' section has helped many people to trace old friends. The association is currently raising funds to place a memorial in the National Memorial Arboretum near Lichfield. It will pay tribute, not just to the evacuees, but to everyone involved in the evacuation, such as the foster parents, teachers, nurses, train drivers and billeting officers.

You can find out more by visiting the ERA website at *www.evacuees. org.uk* or contact the organisation by telephone on 01777 816166.

Index